WHAT TO
DO ABOUT
SMEARING

by the same author

Tom Needs to Go
A book about how to use public toilets safely for boys and
young men with autism and related conditions
Kate E. Reynolds
Illustrated by Jonathon Powell
ISBN 978 1 84905 521 5
eISBN 978 0 85700 935 7

Ellie Needs to Go
A book about how to use public toilets safely for girls and
young women with autism and related conditions
Kate E. Reynolds
Illustrated by Jonathon Powell
ISBN 978 1 84905 524 6
eISBN 978 0 85700 938 8

What's Happening to Tom?
A book about puberty for boys and young men
with autism and related conditions
Kate E. Reynolds
Illustrated by Jonathon Powell
ISBN 978 1 84905 523 9
eISBN 978 0 85700 934 0

What's Happening to Ellie?
A book about puberty for girls and young women
with autism and related conditions
Kate E. Reynolds
Illustrated by Jonathon Powell
ISBN 978 1 84905 526 0
eISBN 978 0 85700 937 1

Things Tom Likes
A book about sexuality and masturbation for boys and
young men with autism and related conditions
Kate E. Reynolds
Illustrated by Jonathon Powell
ISBN 978 1 84905 522 2
eISBN 978 0 85700 933 3

Things Ellie Likes
A book about sexuality and masturbation for girls and
young women with autism and related conditions
Kate E. Reynolds
Illustrated by Jonathon Powell
ISBN 978 1 84905 525 3
eISBN 978 0 85700 936 4

Sexuality and Severe Autism
A Practical Guide for Parents, Caregivers and Health Educators
Kate E. Reynolds
ISBN 978 1 84905 327 3
eISBN 978 0 85700 666 0

Party Planning for Children and Teens on the Autism Spectrum
How to Avoid Meltdowns and Have Fun!
Kate E. Reynolds
ISBN 978 1 84905 277 1
eISBN 978 0 85700 614 1

WHAT TO DO ABOUT SMEARING

A PRACTICAL GUIDE FOR PARENTS AND
CAREGIVERS OF PEOPLE WITH AUTISM,
DEVELOPMENTAL AND INTELLECTUAL
DISABILITIES

Kate E. Reynolds

Illustrations by Lucy Pulleyblank

Jessica Kingsley *Publishers*
London and Philadelphia

The Bristol Stool Form Scale on page 60 is reproduced by kind permission of Dr KW Heaton, Reader in Medicine at the University of Bristol © 2000 Produced by Norgine Pharmaceuticals Limited

First published in 2017
by Jessica Kingsley Publishers
73 Collier Street
London N1 9BE, UK
and
400 Market Street, Suite 400
Philadelphia, PA 19106, USA

www.jkp.com

Library of Congress Cataloging in Publication Data
Title: What to do about smearing : a practical guide for parents and caregivers of people with autism, developmental and intellectual disabilities / Kate E. Reynolds ; illustrations by Lucy Pulleyblank.
Description: London ; Philadelphia : Jessica Kingsley Publishers, 2017. | Includes bibliographical references and index.
Identifiers: LCCN 2016041479 | ISBN 9781785921308 (alk. paper)
Subjects: LCSH: Autistic children--Health and hygiene. | Toilet training. | Developmentally disabled children--Health and hygiene. | Autistic people--Care.
Classification: LCC RJ506.A9 R494 2017 | DDC 618.92/85882--dc23
LC record available at https://lccn.loc.gov/2016041479

British Library Cataloguing in Publication Data
A CIP catalogue record for this book is available from the British Library

ISBN 978 1 78592 130 8
eISBN 978 1 78450 395 6

Printed and bound in Great Britain

To my nephew, Mark Reynolds,
and my nieces, Beth Massam,
Kate Hargreaves,
Jessica Massam,
Emily Massam,
Grace Reynolds
and the late Amy Reynolds,
not forgetting my children, Francesca and Jude,
and my god son Ben Gabriel

Acknowledgements

Thank you to Alice Kemp and all the other parents who gave me their time and shared their personal experiences of smearing with me.

Many thanks to the JKP editorial team, especially my copy editor, Judy Napper, for her immense patience. I hope you still have nails left.

With thanks to my children, Francesca and Jude, who endure my endless hours poring over a computer.

Also thanks to my mother, Sandra Reynolds, for keeping my head above water.

Along with many ex-pupils at the Worcester Grammar School for Girls, I wish to thank my form tutor and French teacher, Mr Jeremy Criddle, for his tremendous sense of humour and teaching skills. We will never forget his sandals, short-sleeved shirts and his penchant for cycling. On a personal note, I also thank him for trying to persuade my parents to buy us a dog, because I was so desperate for one and he had Sadie. He didn't succeed, but I did eventually get my dog – when I was 44!

Contents

Introduction

The impetus for the book

Smearing was brought to my attention when I was researching a previous book and fell upon a series of online conversations among parents and caregivers about the subject. The sense of desperation was palpable and was reflected in the measures people were taking to try to address the problem. A leading strategy seemed to be binding the person who smeared in fitted clothing, often using several layers, with fastenings at the back to prevent access, and wide use of duct tape to seal clothing at the wrists and ankles, and the waist of nappies/diapers. There were also lengthy discussions of how to clean items of faeces and reduce the odour of faeces from a house, which illustrates the social impact of having a person who smears in the home.

Beyond these discussions there appeared to be little knowledge about how to manage smearing and a weary acceptance that smearing was something to be endured. Smearing is an under-researched area and one where assumptions can reinforce the behaviour. For example, there is a myth that smearing is an integral part of having an intellectual disability and, as such, there is very limited potential to improve, minimize or eliminate it.

In *What to Do about Smearing* I examine the current research into this behaviour, which throws up numerous causes of smearing and possible strategies to tackle it. I have also interviewed several parents whose children smear and who appeared to have little support and be resigned to dealing with ongoing smearing. At the end of two interviews I found myself giving basic advice about toilet training and communication skills and wondering where this information should have come from.

In addition, it became clear that eating faeces is sometimes combined with smearing in some individuals. This book will address ingestion of faeces, looking at causes and possible strategies for managing this behaviour.

From writing previous books it's become clear to me that no single book will accurately reflect every reader's experiences. By engaging in broad discussion of the subject of smearing and eating faeces, I hope that all readers will gain insight and strategies to address the issues they face and adapt the information to their personal circumstances.

The current level of research

Smearing behaviour lacks sufficient research into behavioural interventions, and the issue of inappropriate use of faeces is under-researched (Brahm *et al.* 2004). Incontinence and soiling can be assumed to be caused by disability (Smith 1996) and there is an apparent lack of interest in and knowledge of continence issues, reflected in little research in the area, particularly prevention and treatment strategies (Van Laecke 2008). However, there is enough information to form the basis of possible strategies and point to useful future areas for research.

The structure of this book

Chapter 1 consists of the definition of smearing, how common it is and its impact on those around the individual with autism, intellectual and developmental disabilities. In Chapter 2, I discuss the many possible causes of smearing. This leads to the strategies for tackling smearing, which are outlined in Chapter 3. The other faeces-related behaviour I will explore is ingestion or eating faeces, which is covered in Chapter 4. Finally, I discuss what to do if smearing or ingestion of faeces recurs. I have taken the advice of other parents and will use the words 'urine', 'faeces', 'stools' and other 'proper' terminology as opposed to 'pee' and 'poo'. However, this book is designed to be accessible to a range of parents and caregivers, so there is an easy-read summary at the end of each chapter.

Additionally, the book contains examples of visual materials and picture narratives, which have been shown by research to be helpful strategies for some individuals. I use quotes from interviews to illustrate issues for parents and caregivers. Appendix 1 contains information about available support in the UK, the US and Australia.

Definitions

Throughout the book I refer to the person with autism, intellectual and developmental disabilities as 'the individual' for brevity. The following definitions are supplemented by Appendix 2, which contains diagnostic criteria for key medical conditions found in the book.

Autism spectrum disorders/conditions

Until 2014 autism spectrum disorders (ASD) were divided into the following four separate disorders:

- autistic disorder
- Asperger's disorder
- childhood disintegrative disorder
- pervasive developmental disorder not otherwise specified.

This was changed under the new *DSM-5* (*Diagnostic and Statistical Manual of Mental Disorders, Fifth Edition*) criteria which drew together these four disorders into one umbrella term of autism spectrum disorder. It's important to understand the previous criteria for diagnosis because these appear in older texts about autism and often in discussions among parents. The new diagnostic criteria acknowledge the broad range of difficulties involved in autism, from mild to much more severe, specifying that these must have been present since childhood. Challenges for people with autism exist in the following two broad areas:

- limited abilities with communication, which may present as lack of understanding of body language, literal interpretations of spoken language or a history of struggling to create and sustain friendships with their peers of a similar age
- a high dependency on routines in their lives with an almost pathological fear of change, and/ or a focus on objects (often obscure ones) rather than people.

Learning disabilities
This is a wide diagnostic term used in the UK which applies to people with impairments in the following areas:

- an inability or significant challenge to their ability to comprehend new concepts or information and develop new skills

- difficulties in developing life and social skills associated with managing independently.

Both of these criteria must have started in childhood and have an ongoing impact on the person's development. Learning disabilities may warrant the person needing extra support in the community from health and social care, dependent on their social abilities and communication skills, rather than purely their apparent intelligence quotient (IQ). Learning disabilities may be accompanied by physical difficulties and sensory issues but not necessarily. There are multiple causes of learning disabilities, which may include any of the following:

- genetic conditions, such as fragile X syndrome

- chromosomal conditions, for example Down syndrome

- lack of sufficient oxygen at birth, which may cause cerebral palsy

- foetal alcohol syndrome

- extreme abuse or childhood neglect.

Learning disabilities also may accompany autism.

Intellectual disability and intellectual developmental disorder
In 2014 the US term 'mental retardation' was updated to 'intellectual disability' and 'intellectual developmental disorder'. This is very similar to the UK's criteria for learning disabilities but focuses on three areas of impairment:

- difficulties in understanding new concepts and skills involved in language, memorizing, retention of knowledge and academic studies

- challenges with a broad range of social skills, such as lacking communication skills, difficulties creating and maintaining friendships with peers and understanding the social world

- lack of life skills needed for self-care, including issues around managing money, developing personal recreational activities and organizational skills.

Again, difficulties must be identifiable in childhood and have a lasting impact on development.

Increasingly, 'intellectual developmental disorders' and 'intellectual and developmental disabilities' are becoming the global terms for what is referred to in the UK as learning disabilities, so this book will use 'intellectual and developmental disability' and/or 'autism' throughout the text.

Challenging behaviour

The term 'challenging behaviour' may be used to describe faecal smearing and ingesting behaviour. Definitions of challenging behaviours are based on the following:

- The behaviour is not 'normal' for that particular culture: this is important in faecal smearing, which is culturally acceptible in some criminal groups, and pica (ingestion of non-food items) in childen below the age of two (Ali 2001).

- The behaviour constrains the individual's access to the community. Smearing and ingesting faeces may mean that the individual's movements outside the home have to be monitored and restricted.

- The behaviour may injure the individual or others. Ingesting faeces certainly may harm the individual, and smearing potentially may cause physical harm to the individual and others because of the spread of contaminated matter.

Unfortunately, the term 'challenging behaviour' has become moulded into meaning a characteristic of the individual, for example, 'She has challenging behaviour', rather than as a description of a behaviour which might be difficult for families and services to manage (Addison 2013). Smearing and eating faeces may be identified as challenging behaviours, a label which can cause individuals in the UK, at least, to be placed in institutions some distance from their families because local services supposedly can't manage them (Addison 2013).

EASY-READ SUMMARY

I decided to write this book because parents were asking me what to do about their children who were smearing faeces all over the house and themselves. Parents were really upset about this because their home smelled bad and they were worried about taking their child out of the house in case the child smeared faeces somewhere else. This meant that the family didn't get out and do things that other families can do outside the home.

Some parents and other people think that smearing faeces is all part of a disability and nothing can be done about it. In this book I will show that there are lots of reasons why people smear faeces and sometimes eat it. Once I've given the reasons, I will look at how to stop it happening or make it happen less.

1

What Is Smearing?

Definition

Smearing faeces (stools), also referred to as 'scatolia', can include covering objects, such as furniture, walls, carpets and beds, as well as the individual's body. Usually individuals smear their own faeces but they may remove other people's faeces from toilet bowls or others' nappies (diapers), typically, those of younger siblings. Smearing may involve covering siblings and themselves in faeces, including faces, eyes and ears. Other examples of faeces-related behaviours may be:

- rolling pieces of faeces in their hands and then hiding them in their bedroom

- picking up faeces from the toilet bowl to play with or smear

- using an item such as a sock or glove to hold the faeces, then either smearing it or secreting it in chosen places, such as in a shoe or sock

- selecting a specific spot in the house to play with their own faeces

- undressing in the school toilets, removing their clothing, smearing themselves and then replacing their clothes and returning to class
- smearing as part of masturbation
- smearing and shredding nappies/diapers in the same episode
- defecating in the bath and then smearing the tiles, floor and the self.

Possible causes of smearing

Smearing is associated with people who have obsessive compulsive disorder (OCD), anxiety or depressive illness, attention deficit hyperactivity disorder (ADHD), autism spectrum disorders, developmental delays and post-traumatic stress often connected to abuse.

There is research to show that those with more severe forms of autism, developmental and intellectual disabilities are more likely to engage in faecal smearing, although there is no specific intellectual disability in which there is increased likelihood of smearing (Powers 2005). There is evidence that people with disabilities (physical, developmental, intellectual or psychiatric) are up to five times more likely to smear than people without disabilities (Brahm, Farmer and Brown 2007).

Although smearing may not be regarded as a typical behaviour of people with milder forms of autism or intellectual disabilities, it still occurs in this group (Bouras and Drummond 1992). For example, the renowned scientist, speaker and author who has Asperger syndrome, Temple Grandin, smeared faeces in childhood:

> Normal children use clay for modeling; I used my feces and then spread my creations all over the room... I had a violent temper, and when

thwarted, I'd throw anything handy – a museum quality vase or leftover feces. (Grandin and Scariano 1986, p.16)

How common is smearing?

There is no agreement about how commonly smearing is practised. This is partly explained by the fact that very young children – under two years of age – have a fascination with their own faeces, so may play with it as a natural part of growing up. In addition, parents and caregivers may not report smearing for several reasons, including:

- embarrassment that their child behaves this way

- feeling that no other child/young person smears

- not knowing where to go for support

- the feeling that smearing is part of disability and nothing can be done to reduce the behaviour.

Smearing linked to incontinence

Linked to smearing is 'soiling' or faecal incontinence in inappropriate places such as clothing or bedding, after the age when most children are toilet trained – usually by four years old – and can be:

- voluntary (intentional), indicating an underlying psychiatric, psychological/emotional or neurological condition

- involuntary (unintentional), caused by medical conditions, such as constipation.

Smearing is associated in some cases with incontinence of either or both urine and faeces. Incontinence is more common in children and adults with intellectual and developmental disabilities than those developing typically (Von Gontard 2013). Research also has found that children with the following conditions have a greater tendency towards incontinence, which can continue into adulthood if it is not successfully treated in childhood and can be associated with smearing (Von Gontard 2013):

- physical disabilities

- fragile X syndrome

- Rett syndrome

- attention deficit hyperactivity disorder

- Down syndrome

- other conditions associated with a low IQ

- autism.
                        (Fleming and MacAlister 2016)

Psychiatric conditions associated with smearing

The following psychiatric conditions, which may be found alongside intellectual and developmental disabilities, are also linked to smearing behaviour:

- obsessive compulsive disorder

- anxiety disorders

- clinical depression

- schizophrenia

- bipolar disorder

- post-traumatic stress disorder, particularly related to sexual and other abuse.
                        (Ali 2000; Beck and Frohberg 2005;
                        Josephs *et al.* 2016)

Research

Much of the research into smearing has focused on it as a feature of dementia, with far fewer studies of smearing in those with autism and developmental delays (Nagaratnam, Lim and Hutyn 2001). Furthermore, the research that has taken place regarding so-called 'challenging behaviours' appears to have largely failed to thoroughly investigate smearing (Brahm *et al.* 2004). However, results of studies that have been conducted demonstrate that the frequency of smearing can be reduced by using a targeted behavioural approach, outlined below.

How smearing affects the family

Faecal smearing is one of the most common problems with inappropriate behaviours reported by parents (Dalrymple and Ruble 1992). It presents a physical and emotional burden on parents and caregivers and is often in the very place that should be a sanctuary, their home. If this behaviour happens in public, this is even more stressful, due to embarrassment and the unpredictable nature of the behaviour.

> But I went to B&Q [a hardware store] once and...I had tried to get him to the toilet without anybody seeing that my son's hand was covered in poo... We went to a family party and he got into a toilet and took somebody else's poo out of the toilet, playing with it. That was pretty horrible.
>
> Mother of 18-year-old young man with autism, cerebral palsy, intellectual and developmental disabilities

Some parents feel there was no warning of the first episode of smearing, which compounded their shock and disbelief that their child was smearing. Such is the feeling of repulsion and taboo about smearing that parents may hide the fact that their child behaves in this way by avoiding social situations, such as having guests or even employing carers to allow them some respite. The ongoing strain of laundering clothes, bedlinen and other materials such as curtains can exhaust parents. Washing carpets and furniture repeatedly and being conscious of the possibility that the home smells of faeces can also contribute to the negative experience of clearing up after smearing. In addition, parents and caregivers can become emotionally drained and depressed, even to the point of needing medication.

The relationship between parents and their children who smear can be severely affected, with some parents feeling that their child is smearing as an act of aggression or spite. This can feel like a direct attack on the parent, and the longer the behaviour continues the more corrosive the effect may be on the bond between parents and their children.

Parents may feel their children are the only ones to engage in smearing, a response which is only reinforced by a general lack of discussion of the subject. It may be difficult for parents to seek advice from professionals because of embarrassment or a feeling that their parenting may be criticized. In addition, if parents have looked at information about smearing, they may be concerned that professionals may believe that there has been child abuse in the family, since this is one area that is covered in generally available information about smearing.

Another cause of distress is the process of cleaning the child, which may involves wiping his face and eyes. There may be faeces in the child's mouth or teeth, or embedded in fingernails, which parents report as a repulsive cleaning experience.

Having a sibling who smears causes immense anxiety to other children in the family, who cannot invite friends home in case the house smells of faeces or their sibling smears in front of friends. Smearing is difficult enough for parents and caregivers to understand and manage but it is extraordinarily hard to explain this behaviour to others from outside the family. In turn, other children in the family become isolated in line with their parents. Some siblings may develop a deep-seated anger towards the smearer, whose behaviour may dominate the household and monopolize much of the attention of parents.

There is also the health risk to others in the home, where traces of faeces may be left on door handles, cutlery or other household items and can spread infection (Rolider *et al.* 1991). There can be some sense of urgency around trying to address such behaviours because of the concerns around hygiene and infection, which can cause inappropriate punishment by parents and caregivers (Rolider *et al.* 1991).

How smearing affects the individual

Smearing may affect the individual's ability to go on school trips or stay at other people's homes, such as relatives. Ultimately, in common with other socially problematic behaviours, individuals who smear may have their freedom in the community severely limited. Yet all these experiences are important for developing communication skills and having varied life experiences, the lack of which may cause smearing to happen in the first place.

Smearing, if it persists, may cause parents both physical and emotional exhaustion and a level of emotional distance from their child. For some parents, this may lead to them placing their children in residential care, which may be geographically distant from the family home. This eventuality may not be apparent to the individual, who may not have the cognitive abilities to anticipate future consequences but who needs family contact and support.

Faecal smearing can cause serious health issues for the individual, as explained in later chapters.

EASY-READ SUMMARY

Some individuals with autism and intellectual (learning) disabilities smear their own or other people's faeces. They may wipe faeces over things in the house, such as the carpet or walls. This can upset parents and caregivers because of the smell in the home and having to clean up faeces. Smearing faeces also makes it hard to take people who do the smearing out to shops, the cinema or other places outside the home, in case the person smears faeces. Parents and the rest of the family may feel very alone because they can't invite friends or other people to the house in case smearing happens. They may not be able to talk to other people about smearing because they don't know which doctors or other professionals know about smearing and they are worried about what other people might think about the person doing the smearing.

There are many things that cause people to smear. People who have certain conditions, like autism, depression and anxiety problems, are more likely to smear. Smearing also happens more when someone wets or soils himself regularly, which happens more with some conditions, such as ADHD and Down syndrome.

This doesn't mean that everyone with these conditions will smear: it just means that studies show people who smear are more likely to have these conditions. But anyone can smear.

The best way to decrease or stop smearing is to work out why smearing happens in the first place. The person doing the smearing may get good things from doing it, such as attention from other people, even if this is a parent being angry. Or it may stop other people being around when the person who smears wants to be alone for a while. Other reasons for smearing may be that the person likes the feel and warmth of faeces and this may make him feel nice inside and is something he wants to do over again.

Unfortunately, smearing can mean that the person has to stay at home most or all of the time in case he smears. It can get so hard for the family that the person may be placed in care away from home. Smearing can also cause the person to be ill with different infections.

All of these things are explained more in the chapters in this book.

2

Causes of Smearing

It is only through understanding that there are many causes of smearing that effective strategies can be developed to address it. Sometimes there is more than one cause of smearing in one individual, making reducing and resolving the behaviour more complex.

Causes of smearing may include one or more of the following:

- medical issues, such as gastrointestinal disease (Brahm *et al.* 2004)

- psychiatric issues

- sensory stimulation (Prasher and Clarke 1996)

- emotional causes, such as trying to escape a situation (Friedin and Johnson 1979) and aggression (Brahm *et al.* 2007)

- sexual, emotional and physical abuse (Bernard 1999; Sinason 2002)

- dietary factors (Kral *et al.* 2013).

Medical issues

The first step towards identifying the causes of smearing is to eliminate medical reasons. Faecal smearing warrants referral for a gastrointestinal or genitourinary medical opinion, depending on symptoms. The consultant should conduct a careful medical assessment with investigations to detect any underlying conditions (Powers 2005).

Assumptions surrounding intellectual and developmental disabilities include a myth that certain medical conditions are inevitable, such as constipation, which is linked to smearing.

> I thought it [abdominal pain] could be because he was premature, he was just behind. Then our doctor said that children with autism suffer from constipation. Now we have a new doctor and I feel someone is listening to me. I feel there's something more going on because he's always got pain...in his bowel... That is why I know it's not just because he's autistic – it's because there's something wrong. The doctor has listened to me and they're going to get him a scan...and it's because he's in so much pain and if he doesn't go he's sick.
>
> Mother of four-year-old boy with autism and intellectual and developmental disabilities

Parents and caregivers often act as advocates for people with intellectual and developmental disabilities to ensure satisfactory medical assessment and treatment. Disturbingly, recent research has shown that death rates among people with intellectual disabilities were two and a half times higher than in the general population (Heslop *et al.* 2013). In addition, research focusing on autism found that people with autism and intellectual disabilities die more than 30 years prematurely, with an average age of 39 years (Cusack *et al.* 2016).

Constipation

Faecal constipation is defined as having bowel movements that are infrequent – less than three times per week – and difficult or painful to pass. Research into constipation in people with intellectual and developmental disabilities estimates that anything between 26 and 69 per cent of them have constipation compared with the general population (Bohmer *et al.* 2001; Sullivan 2008). One study found that 74 per cent of children with cerebral palsy at a specialist outpatients clinic had chronic (ongoing) constipation (Del Giudice *et al.* 1999). Yet constipation may be missed by doctors initially, in part because constipation is more common than they realize (Coleman and Spurling 2010).

Individuals with intellectual and developmental disabilities can all be affected by factors that cause constipation in the general population, such as dehydration and lack of fibre in the diet. However, some conditions make individuals more prone to constipation. For example, people with Down syndrome have a greater likelihood of having the following disorders, all of which can cause constipation:

- Hypothyroidism: this is when the metabolic rate is lower than usual, causing the person to feel sluggish and fatigued, gain weight and be prone to constipation.

- Hirschsprung's disease: this condition mainly affects the colon (large bowel leading to the rectum), causing gastrointestinal problems including chronic constipation, diarrhoea, vomiting and a swollen abdomen.

- Coeliac disease: coeliac disease is a relatively common gastrointestinal condition which is caused by an autoimmune response to gluten in the diet and can cause constipation or diarrhoea.

People with autism spectrum disorders may also have gastrointestinal problems. These can cause diarrhoea and/or constipation. Chronic constipation can lead to intractable nausea, loss of appetite, abdominal pain and a general feeling of being unwell. This can start at an early age.

> The first episode was so long ago. She was earlier than 19 months old. She would hold on until we got home – she's still on Movicol now – and I thought she was holding on and smearing it because she felt that she was achieving something. It would hurt and she would cry, it was really early on, she'd be in the cot, and you'd have to not put babygrows on her, you'd have to put sleep suits...so she couldn't get into her nappy. But it happened at a really early age.
>
> Mother of eight-year-old girl with autism, epilepsy, intellectual and developmental disabilities

WHY IS CONSTIPATION COMMONLY ASSOCIATED WITH DISABILITY?

Constipation is more common in people with intellectual, developmental and physical disabilities for several reasons.

- Physical activity is an important part of stimulating gut activity to move faeces effectively through the bowel. People with disabilities may be less likely to be physically active, sometimes through physical disability, sometimes through lack of understanding and motivation to exercise, and sometimes medications may contribute to people with disabilities gaining weight and feeling less able to do exercise. In addition, low expectations of what they can achieve physically may prevent people with disabilities from regularly exercising.

- Lack of fluids. Unless an individual is able to request a drink, this aspect of their support may be neglected. In addition, research on children shows that some parents and caregivers may restrict fluids to prevent urinary incontinence, which has the negative effect of reducing bladder capacity in children and is directly related to constipation (Van Laecke 2008). Although there is some advice to reduce fluids towards bedtime for some children and adults with night-time incontinence (Fleming and MacAlister 2016), this is not advice which should be applied generally throughout the day. In the UK the National Institute for Clinical Excellence (NICE) recommends children and young people should drink between 1200 ml of fluid for 4–8-year-old children, up to 1800 ml for young women aged 14–18 years and 2600 ml for young men aged 14–18 years (NICE 2010).

  Dehydration contributes to constipation because there is insufficient softness to the stools for them to be squeezed through the bowel. In addition, if the individual starts to become constipated, faeces become stuck in the large bowel, which has a major function of reabsorbing fluid from stools, to prevent dehydration in the body. However, if the person is not consuming enough fluid, stools remain in the bowel, moving slowly through, and fluid is continuously reabsorbed from solid stools which become increasingly hard.

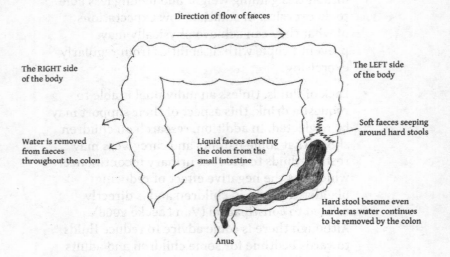

Direction of flow of faeces

The RIGHT side of the body

The LEFT side of the body

Water is removed from faeces throughout the colon

Liquid faeces entering the colon from the small intestine

Soft faeces seeping around hard stools

Hard stool besome even harder as water continues to be removed by the colon

Anus

FIGURE 2.1 THE CONSTIPATED LARGE INTESTINE (COLON)

- Limited diet. Sensory issues for those with autism may impact on their diet, with some people restricting their food to items that feel comfortable on their palate, which may be only soft foods. For others, sensory factors may cause them to eat only bland-coloured foods. So some people may not have sufficient roughage or fibre in their daily intake of food, an element which is extremely important in the gastrointestinal system because fibre is not broken down and absorbed by the body but helps bulk out stools to help their passage through the bowel. Other people with intellectual and developmental disabilities may refuse to eat (Coleman and Spurling 2010).

- People with intellectual and developmental disabilities may have issues surrounding using the toilet.

- Certain medications which are more widely prescribed in populations of people with intellectual and developmental disabilities may cause or increase the potential for constipation, including anticonvulsants, benzodiazepines and antipsychotics (Bohmer *et al.* 2001).

- Additionally, people with intellectual and developmental disabilities may lack bowel tone, which affects the ability to squeeze faeces through the bowel efficiently, resulting in constipation and even faecal obstruction.

- Constipation initially can be caused by a child experiencing pain when trying to pass hard faeces. This can lead to reluctance to use the toilet for a bowel movement, possibly creating a cycle which perpetuates constipation.

- Children may hold their faeces for emotional reasons, such as anxiety, fear or unwillingness or difficulty using toilets with which they are unfamiliar.

> When she gets anxious she just will not release poo. So she can go for days without going, you can see her belly getting bigger and you're just rubbing her belly and rubbing her back, until she destresses. It could be the simplest thing like somebody at school looks at her the wrong way, that tiny little thing is a big issue.
>
> Mother of eight-year-old girl with autism, epilepsy, intellectual and developmental disabilities

- Chronic constipation may decrease the bowel sensations so the child cannot perceive when she needs the toilet. In turn, this may lead to the child soiling her underwear, with all the embarrassment and stigma this can cause.

- Finally, parents, caregivers and doctors may not identify the signs of constipation in individuals, partly due to difficulties with communication. The individual may sleep poorly, seem non-specifically distressed, be aggressive, self-harm or have changes in behaviour, all of which may seem unconnected to bowel activity (Carr and Smith 1995; Coleman and Spurling 2010). Behaviours such as insomnia or a level of aggression may not be unusual in the individual or may be accepted by the parent, caregiver and even professionals as being part of having a disability. If the child is mobile enough to use the toilet without support and flushes it, parents and caregivers may be unaware that the child is becoming constipated.

CONSTIPATION LEADING TO SMEARING

The individual is likely to have abdominal discomfort or pain which she may find is relieved by removing faeces from the rectum by hand. Additionally, solid stools in the bowel may be bypassed by fluid faeces, which seep past hard stools and cause soiling. This so-called 'overflow' soiling may look like diarrhoea but is actually a sign of constipation.

A full, constipated bowel can also press on the bladder and cause urinary incontinence. This can cause soiling or leaking urine in underwear and an uncomfortable or itchy perianal area (the area between the anus and the vagina in women or testicles in men). In turn this can lead to the individual poking the anus or scratching the perianal area; and if she reaches hard stools, she may become fascinated by playing with faeces.

If the child tries to clean herself after leaking faeces in her underwear, she may not manage well, and seem to be smearing when she is not.

Smearing, faecal and urinary incontinence can lead to further social stigma for the individual, which may already exist because of her intellectual and developmental disability (Coleman and Spurling 2010).

According to research, treating constipation in children with disabilities is frequently delayed for months and even years (Elawad and Sullivan 2001). More disturbing is that evidence suggests that when people with intellectual disabilities die in hospital of intestinal obstruction, this is often because of constipation which has not been brought to medical attention until it is very severe (Jancar and Speller 1994).

Communication difficulties are a key reason for delays in diagnoses and must be a continuous priority in supporting people with intellectual and developmental disabilities. Medical practitioners may need parents and caregivers to advocate for the individual to help identify symptoms, such as levels of pain, which may be key to diagnosing conditions.

Anal itching

Anal itching (or *pruritus ani*) has multiple causes and is a cause of anal poking, scratching and smearing.

The anal area can become inflamed, meaning that the individual may 'dig' at her anus to relieve the itching or pain. Itching can become intense and the skin even more inflamed as a direct result of scratching and the moisture that is present in the perianal area. Itching can be caused by any of the following:

- A reaction to chemicals in faeces, including waste products associated with certain foods, such as spicy hot sauces, chilli peppers, citrus fruits, nuts, chocolate, dairy products and coffee (Jones 1992).

- Pinworms, which are parasitic worms that infect the intestines. They are spread when people ingest pinworm eggs, which may be found on contaminated surfaces of furnishings, food and drinking utensils, and garments such as underwear. They are the most common worms that affect children, but other types also cause anal itching.

- Protozoal infections and other bowel infections such as cryptosporidiosis and campylobacter, which can all cause diarrhoea. In turn, the inflammation around the anus can cause the person to dig rectally to relieve itching and inflammation (Brahm et al. 2004).

- Sexually transmitted infections.

- Skin conditions, such as psoriasis (similar to eczema) and cancer.

- Cancers located in the anus or bowel.

- Yeast infections, often caused by a moist anal area or sometimes antibiotics.

- Overflow diarrhoea, or leaking from the anus, causing it to be moist.

- Haemorrhoids, rectal prolapse and other rectal disorders (see below).

- Tears around the anal opening (called fissures), which can become infected.

- Conditions such as Crohn's disease, which can cause pathways, or fistulas, to form, which allow fluids down to the anus which should not be there and which cause irritation.

- Conditions affecting the entire body, such as diabetes, anaemia, lymphomas and jaundice.

- Faecal incontinence caused by lack of toileting skills, certain medications or sexual abuse.

Anal itching can cause interruptions to sleep and unbearable irritation which may be felt as burning. It can affect every part of a person's life because it is so intolerable and it could be displayed in so-called challenging behaviours. Treatment requires intervention by a family doctor and referral to a specialist, usually a gastroenterologist. The consultant will examine the anus for visual abnormalities, and may put a finger into the anus to identify haemorrhoids or possibly a tumour. A proctoscopy may be performed, where a tube is inserted into the anus which the consultant can look through to see obvious medical issues. Pinworms and their eggs can be tested for, using a special tape at the anal opening to which they adhere.

Haemorrhoids

Haemorrhoids (piles) are swollen and inflamed veins in the anus and the lower part of the rectum. They can result from straining on the toilet, trying to open the bowels when the individual is constipated. The pain of haemorrhoids and straining may prevent the child from fully emptying her bowels, increasing the constipation. Haemorrhoids are itchy and painful, so she may scratch and 'dig' around the anal area. The child may find that manually removing faeces relieves some of the pain and discomfort.

Rectal prolapse

Chronic constipation and straining to empty the bowels can cause the child to have a rectal prolapse. This is when the rectum (the last part of the bowel leading to the anal opening) slips out of its position and can be pushed out through the anus. It looks like a bunch of black grapes if fully prolapsed, but may partially prolapse. Faecal incontinence and a feeling that the bowel is not fully emptied result and this can lead to faecal smearing.

In addition to constipation, contributing factors to rectal prolapse in children with autism and intellectual disabilities include the following conditions:

- Ehlers-Danlos syndrome

- Hirschsprung's disease

- malnutrition

- psychiatric disease

- parasitic infections

- anything that causes pressure in the abdomen, such as constipation, severe and chronic cough and obesity.

Genitourinary issues

Smearing may be caused by genitourinary issues, that is, something associated with the bladder, kidneys and urinary tract and/or the genitals (Brahm et al. 2004). Urinary tract infections may occur in individuals with intellectual and developmental disabilities and autism owing to being under-hydrated because:

- they cannot access their own drinks

- parents and caregivers may erroneously limit fluids to prevent them wetting themselves or to prevent wet nappies/diapers

- they may lack communication skills to request a drink

- restrictive clothing can cause them to sweat profusely.

Urinary tract infections, particularly in women or girls, can cause urinary incontinence and the perianal area to become inflamed and itchy. If left untreated, the infection could backtrack, causing kidney infection.

Women and girls also may have perianal discomfort as a result of sexually transmissible infections, vaginitis (inflammation of the vagina and vaginal entrance) or vulvitis (inflammation of the vulva, the external genitals).

Feeling uncomfortable may cause a woman to scratch or 'dig' at the perianal area to relieve the itch or discomfort. In doing so, women and girls may start to reach into the anus or anal entrance and retrieve faeces, which they then may smear to remove it from their fingers. The process of digitally rubbing the perianal and anal areas may cause infections in the vagina or excoriated areas of the vulva because faecal matter is passed from the anal canal.

Urinary incontinence

Studies of children with intellectual and developmental disabilities put the prevalence of urinary incontinence (the uncontrollable leaking of urine) at anything from 23 to 86 per cent (Van Laecke 2008). Again, there are numerous causes of incontinence of urine, including:

- reduced bladder capacity: reported to occur in over 70 per cent of people with intellectual disability in one study (Van Laecke 2008)

- overactive bladder

- physical difficulties with the mechanics of urinating

- trying to avoid urination, perhaps because the individual is distracted with something else

- stress incontinence caused when the bladder is under pressure, for example when the individual is coughing or laughing.

Many of these may be addressed medically. It is important that children and adults with urinary incontinence are referred for medical assessment and treatment, partly to enhance their quality of life but also because urinary incontinence is related to other behaviours such as smearing.

Issues for ageing people with intellectual/ developmental disabilities and autism

Older women who are perimenopausal (the transition period of an average four years leading to menopause) or menopausal may experience itching in the perineal area (between the vaginal opening and the anus) as their oestrogen levels dip. The skin of the vulva may also thin with the menopause, allowing it to be damaged more easily and open to infection in general and from the anus.

The incidence of uterine fibroids increases in women with age, affecting more than 30 per cent of women aged 40 to 60 years (Evans and Brunsell 2007). Fibroids are benign growths which can cause pain and bleeding. Conditions which cause prolonged periods of bleeding can cause the perianal area to be constantly damp and itchy or prone to infection.

These factors can cause the woman to scratch and 'dig' at the area, sometimes exploring further to the anal canal and its contents. This may have particular significance for women with Down syndrome, who tend to have earlier menopausal experiences than typically developed women (Schupf *et al.* 1997).

In older men the prostate commonly enlarges, regardless of intellectual and developmental disability. As the prostate gets bigger it can press on the bladder, causing difficulties with urinating and urine infections from urine remaining in the bladder without being able to fully empty it. Discomfort and possible urinary infections may cause the man to 'dig' in the perineal area to try to relieve the feeling. Again, this may lead to exploration of the anus (Powers 2005).

Psychiatric conditions

Obsessive compulsive disorder

Smearing may be related to self-stimulatory behaviours, which are used by individuals to achieve a level of sensory input that they lack due to autism, intellectual and developmental disabilities. In psychiatric terms, smearing and ingesting faeces may be regarded as an obsessive compulsive condition.

Clinical depression

Clinical depression can be one of the conditions that contributes to so-called psychological anal itching where there is no physical or medical problem with the anus or surrounding area. Instead, the feeling of itchiness and the need to scratch is psychosomatic (caused or worsened by the mind, such as through stress or internal conflict) or the result of psychiatric conditions (relating to mental illness, such as anxiety disorders) (NICE 2014).

Insomnia

Insomnia is a chronic disorder which causes the individual to find it difficult to fall asleep, stay asleep or can involve waking early and being unable to return to sleep.

These disturbed sleep patterns can contribute to smearing behaviours because the individual may wake and engage in smearing due to boredom, loneliness or habit when alone in bed.

Oppositional defiant disorder

Individuals with oppositional defiant disorder (ODD) may engage in power struggles with parents and caregivers over toilet training and may voluntarily soil themselves. The condition causes the individual to display anger/irritation in argumentative and confrontational or defiant ways (see Appendix 2 for diagnostic criteria). The effects of ODD can be exaggerated if the individual has other conditions, notably attention deficit disorders with or without hyperactivity (ADHD and attention deficit disorder (ADD)) and depression (Dickstein 2010).

Conduct disorder

ADHD is most frequently associated with conduct disorder (see Appendix 2 for diagnostic criteria), anxiety and depressive disorders and is one of the most common psychiatric conditions of children and young people (Turgay 2005). Individuals with conduct disorder with ADHD present with hyperactivity and impulsivity plus severe aggression, all of which can combine to make toileting skills difficult to teach. These conditions are often combined with other conditions (called comorbidity), which should be diagnosed by a psychiatrist.

Pathological demand avoidance

Pathological demand avoidance (PDA) is accepted to be part of the autism spectrum. In addition to challenges affecting social interaction and communication, over-dependence on routines and intense interest in inappropriate objects, people with PDA strenuously avoid social demands and expectations, driven by a pathological need to be in control as a means of containing extreme anxiety. These features can make teaching toilet skills difficult.

Exposure anxiety

Anxiety-based conditions are common in individuals with intellectual and developmental disabilities. Exposure anxiety occurs when the individual has extreme responses to social contact and human proximity, because of an acutely self-conscious mindset (Williams 2002). The theory is that smearing, being socially unacceptable and provoking negative emotions in parents and caregivers, reduces people intruding into the lives of individuals. Smearing therefore becomes a positive behaviour for the individual because it results in desired outcomes: fewer episodes of human contact, which cause the individual such distress.

Sensory factors

Individuals with intellectual and developmental disabilities and autism may have sensory integration dysfunction (SID), which occurs when the individual has difficulty processing information. Typically developing individuals receive sensory input from all five senses:

- visual (sight)
- tactile (touch)
- auditory (hearing)
- olfactory (smell)
- gustatory (taste).

This sensory information is integrated to allow the individual to make sense of the world and respond to new experiences (Prasher and Clarke 1996).

SID can affect individuals by making them over-sensitive to sensory input, so they may feel overwhelmed by noise, sights, smells and touch, such as the sound of the toilet being flushed, the smell of bleach and the texture of toilet paper, which the individual may feel as rough. This is important in the context of developing toileting skills when different stimuli in bathrooms and toilets may interfere with the individual's ability to focus on the tasks of using the toilet.

Some individuals have low sensory responses so they attempt to instil sensory input through self-stimulatory behaviours. For example, the individual may rock back and forth, head-bang, jump or clap. In terms of smearing, the individual may seek certain textures, such as the slimy, slick feel of a piece of faeces, as well as the warm temperature giving satisfaction. Some individuals may enjoy the sensation of a soiled nappy/diaper or underwear. Not only is the sense of touch satisfied by smearing but the smell can give much-wanted olfactory (nasal) stimulation.

> I think it was [a sensory thing]. I think he liked sitting in a squidgy pile of poo... Perhaps that's why he never wanted to toilet train because he liked it in his pants. I certainly think he didn't mind the sensation of having it against his skin even at the age of four when he was certainly aware of what was going on... He wouldn't tell me, he'd just walk around... I mean we went to a wedding long after he was toilet trained – he must've been six – and he was walking around at the front of the church and I looked at him and I thought 'He's walking like John Wayne' so I called him over and I said, 'You've pooed yourself, what's going on? You're toilet trained, you haven't pooed yourself for two years.' I think it's because he knew there was no toilet in church so therefore he had no choice,

> but instead of coming over to me – 'Mum I've got a problem' – he just pooed himself and carried on walking around.
>
> Mother of seven-year-old boy with autism and ADHD, who had smeared when he was aged four

Sensory integration dysfunction can also interfere with the individual's awareness of physical signals indicating that they have a full bowel (or bladder) and need to use the toilet. In addition, some individuals may not comprehend that they are wet or have soiled their nappy/ diaper or underwear. For those with heightened sensory input, they may experience faeces moving through the bowel as more uncomfortable than typically developing people, and even distressing.

Other issues with teaching toilet skills

Other features of having autism and/or intellectual and developmental disabilities may contribute to issues around developing toilet training skills:

- Anxiety issues, such as being anxious about using the toilet, for example, being afraid of being physically unstable on the toilet or anxiety that someone unexpectedly will walk in through the toilet door. Some individuals may fear dripping urine on themselves and dislike the sensation of dampness.

- Communication issues: some individuals may not understand verbal language and need symbols, signs or other visual techniques to know what is happening and what's expected of them. Some may not be aware that they can initiate using the toilet by asking to go, using symbols, signs or key words. Whatever form of communication is used, it can only be effective in developing toilet skills if it is consistent across environments, such as school and home. In addition, people with autism may be literal and do precisely what they are asked, such as the classic request to 'put the toilet roll down the toilet' resulting in the entire roll being put in!

- Lack of social awareness: individuals often do not have social networks and friendships in which typically developing children learn and sometimes are competitive. So they don't have the impetus to start wearing underpants instead of nappies/diapers and they don't have conversations around toilet skills or other intimate subjects which typically developing children do.

- Lack of motor skills: using the toilet effectively means that the individual needs to be able to pull her clothes up and down and lower herself onto the toilet seat. Additionally, it requires an ability to turn the torso around to wipe the anal area, an action which may need to be repeated several times until the anus is completely clean. The individual may be thought to have smeared when she has made unsuccessful efforts to clean herself. Beyond this, the individual needs to be able to stand up again, replace her clothing and then wash her hands. All these actions require fine and gross motor skills which she may lack or need practice to use effectively.

- Challenges with transitions: individuals with ADHD, autism, pathological demand avoidance and other intellectual and developmental disabilities tend to have difficulties with transitions from one situation to another (Fleming and MacAlister 2016). This is pertinent for toilet training skills because individuals have to move from one activity, which they may be engaged in and enjoying, to using the toilet, which they may find anxiety-raising.

- If the individual becomes bored while using the toilet, she may fail to empty her bowel fully and this may lead to the bowels opening while the individual is in bed and relaxed.

- The pleasure derived from smearing may be immense and coupled with a commensurate lack of understanding of the feelings of others and the distress the behaviour is having on them. Some parents and caregivers may attempt to demonstrate their distress, even disgust, through emotional explosions, anger or sometimes punishment for the behaviour. But such responses can actually feed the behaviour, although they may give temporary release for parents and caregivers.

He'd taken off his PJs and nappy and done a poo on the carpet, and a wee under the bed and on his bear and a bit more by the window and on the curtain and some clothes. Then while I was cleaning that up, A [his sister] decided she couldn't bear the poo and was sick all over her bed, including the sheet, undersheet, duvet and bear! Aaargh! It was just too much and I ended up crying my eyes out and being pathetic and shouting at B, who kept getting off the bed and giggling... When he saw me crying he was so sweet and hugged me and said sorry and he wouldn't do it again – but he always says that and it never happens! He wouldn't sit still and carried on jumping about and giggling, and I'm so ashamed but I really lost it and smacked him hard on the thigh so he cried – but even then he stopped almost immediately and laughed again – he just doesn't get it! I feel so awful – it's like I'm trying to get a reaction from him but he just can't seem to understand that his behaviour is bad, or I'm cross, or whatever! I'm just grateful that despite my shouting at him for half an hour or so – all the time I was cleaning, every time he got off the bed – and smacking him hard, he still laughs and is happy and loves me! I don't deserve it!

Mother of seven-year-old boy with autism and ADHD, who had smeared when he was aged four

Attitudes of parents and caregivers are key to supporting individuals:

- Problems associated with teaching toilet skills are sometimes derived from unrealistic expectations of what individuals should manage. This may be expecting developmental skills in line with typically developing children/adults. Conversely, very low expectations can 'disable' individuals, ensuring that some remain in nappies/diapers beyond that which is necessary and without attempting the basics of training in toilet skills.

- Some parent and caregivers may view individuals as avoiding using the toilet if they attempt to postpone urination or defecation by, say, hopping from foot to foot, visibly squeezing or kneeling down with their heel at their anus through clothing. This, in fact, is a critical part of learning continence and it is at this point that the individual needs to have adequate communication skills to ask for the toilet. Being able to contain urine and faeces temporarily is a vital toileting skill.

- Like typically developing children, individuals may seek a quiet, familiar spot to go to the toilet such as behind a sofa or behind a door to use a nappy/diaper. Some parents may find it disheartening to see this repeated activity. However, individuals are demonstrating awareness of the need to defecate and the ability to hold it until they are in a comfortable place for them, which are two important aspects of being ready to learn further toilet training skills. This also outlines the need to change nappies/diapers in the bathroom or toilet so that the individual associates those rooms with bowel actions and urinating.

- Some parents and caregivers may consider smearing to be an act of manipulation. If individuals have few communication skills, the only means open to them may be to use actions to achieve something they cannot verbally express or express through symbols and signs. Smearing, in this sense, is a form of communication, even if it sometimes feels like a form of manipulation to parents and caregivers, causing feelings of resentment and anger.

- Other parents and caregivers perceive smearing as an act of revenge. Individuals with autism, intellectual and developmental disabilities have difficulty understanding consequences or being able to comprehend the concept of future. To do an act of revenge a person has to understand these challenging concepts; indeed, much of our work with individuals is designed to help them appreciate consequences, using Social Stories™, for example (Gray 2010).

- Some parents and caregivers may feel that it is inappropriate or unrealistic to allow the individual any level of autonomy or choice in what is happening in her life. Faecal smearing may be the only way individuals can exert any level of control over their lives, giving them a sense of power which they lack in all other aspects of their lives (Williams 2002).

Dietary factors

Individuals with autism in particular may find their diet very self-limited with very few items being eaten, and these often being highly specific. For example, sausages may be eaten but only one brand. This tends to be for sensory reasons, so the individual may only eat smooth foods, and nothing with a crisp edge like toast or roast potatoes. Sometimes the individual will only eat one colour of food (often bland), so a typical plate of food might be boiled potatoes, butter beans and an egg – and the individual may insist that none of the foods touch each other on the plate. Once attached to one food, it may be difficult to move the individual on to other foods. Unfortunately, foods of choice may not be as fibrous or nutritious as is necessary to help maintain regular bowel movements, which can lead to constipation.

Emotional factors

Emotional factors can contribute to smearing and may be any or many of the following:

- Soiling may cause frustration in individuals, who smear as a result.

- Smearing may be a way of expressing frustration, helplessness and powerlessness.

- An individual may smear as a means of getting attention, whether positive or negative. The behaviour can result in immediate responses which divert attention from other siblings, family members or activities. The attention acts as a reward and the individual may be encouraged to engage further in smearing.

- An individual may have learned that she gets positive rewards, even inadvertently, by smearing, such as a hot bath.

- Smearing may occur as a response to anxiety, such as a change to the individual's routine, changes in staff caring for the individual, or a friend leaving shared supported living arrangements.

- Individuals may feel the need for some sense of autonomy: smearing may be the only time they can experience control over any aspect of their lives.

> For him it is something that he controls. He can choose to do it and I think with P there's always been massive issues about control, so he can choose to use it or not.
>
> Mother of 18-year-old young man with autism, cerebral palsy, Ehlers-Danlos syndrome, intellectual and developmental disabilities

- Under-stimulation or boredom can be a cause of smearing, especially at night when there are no distractions.

- Expressing anger: the individual may not have learned how to express anger in appropriate ways, due to lack of communication skills, for example. Smearing may act as a channel for anger and helplessness which the individual cannot otherwise express, and can give some level of power over the parents and caregivers in her life.

Sexual factors

Sexual gratification

Individuals may explore their own bodies sexually from early childhood. This behaviour can give them comfort as well as immense excitement and relief of frustrations and sexual tension. The area around the anus is sensitive and the individual may find this sexually stimulating (Reynolds 2013).

Additionally, there have been cases when masturbation takes place in the presence of soft and fluid faeces, which may be used as a lubricant (Case and Konstantareas 2011; personal communication 2015). This has clear implications for possible infection by passing micro-organisms from the anus into the vagina or the tip of the penis.

> Yes, it [smearing] really gets him going [sexually].
> Mother of 19-year-old young man with autism, and intellectual and developmental disabilities

Smearing may be associated with comforting emotional and sensory experiences and may be a comforting ritual.

Sexual and other abuse

Sometimes soiling may be an indication of penetrative anal intercourse. Research on children has shown that soiling can result from sexual abuse regardless of penetrative or non-penetrative sexual acts perpetrated on the individual (Mellon, Whiteside and Freidrich 1990). Soiling in this circumstance is one of many stress-induced behaviours which can present after sexual abuse, which may include tasting and ingesting faeces and urine (Warnke 1991).

Not only sexual but also serious physical abuse, such as beatings, can cause the individual to be emotionally detached from sensations below the waist. The individual becomes unable to recognize signals to open her bowels, leading to soiling.

Emotional or psychological abuse may involve humiliating, ignoring or sometimes isolating individuals and can result in soiling, which can lead to further humiliation from perpetrators and immense anxiety in the individual about future episodes of soiling. Emotional abuse usually exists alongside other forms of abuse or neglect of basic care (Radford *et al.* 2011).

Soiling and sexual penetration of the anus are linked to smearing behaviour, as previously mentioned, as they can cause inflammation and itching which draws the individual to touch, rub and scratch the anus. In addition, sexual abuse may cause sexually transmissible diseases, which may cause anal/vaginal discharge and inflammatory reactions.

Smearing may be a way of trying to make sense of whatever violations or sexual abuse have happened to the individual. Whether a child or adult, the individual may not be able to express her feelings about everything that has occurred, so smearing acts as an outlet for her distress.

Finally, smearing may be used by the individual to deter the perpetrator by disgusting them with the behaviour. If the individual is successful in preventing an episode of sexual abuse by smearing faeces, the individual may repeat the smearing behaviour as a form of personal protection.

EASY-READ SUMMARY

Smearing has five main causes. The first is physical problems, like piles or constipation, which cause the area near the bottom hole to be wet or itchy, so the person scratches and pokes fingers up the hole. The person may then try to rub off the faeces, often on whatever is near, like curtains or bedding. Constipation is a large problem when the person has a bowel motion less than three times each week, so faeces get stuck in the bowels, getting harder and harder all the time. Some medicines, little exercise and fluid intake, not enough fibre in food and some conditions can cause constipation or make it worse.

Some people like the feel of faeces and its strong smell and enjoy playing with it. There are different things that can be used instead of faeces, like play dough or creams, which the person might enjoy and don't cause illnesses like faeces can.

A person may be treated badly by families or caregivers, perhaps because she has a disability, and this can make the person smear because she is upset.

Problems with mental health also can cause the person to smear or can make it worse. Some conditions make the person less able to learn how to use toilets or be scared of using toilets, and others make smearing something that the person enjoys. Some people show their feelings by smearing, for instance if they're bored or angry.

Smearing can result when a person has been forced to have sex, either as a child or adult.

Sometimes a person can enjoy the feeling of touching their bottom hole.

3

How to Manage Smearing

Aims of interventions

Many parents and caregivers feel worn out physically and emotionally from crisis-managing episode after episode of smearing. Parents and caregivers need support and encouragement from professionals to understand and help develop the individual's toilet skills, which is one of the first steps towards diminishing or stopping smearing, after excluding medical or psychiatric causes. A useful reference for professionals is Fleming and MacAlister's thorough and accessible book about toilet training (Fleming and MacAlister 2016).

It is important not to accept smearing as an integral part of disability but to tackle it on an individual level as an issue that can be addressed in a positive way.

> The attitude was 'Well, you just have to live with it, really.'
>
> Mother of 18-year-old young man with autism, cerebral palsy, intellectual and developmental disabilities

Low-arousal responses described below and trying to be as unemotional as possible will enable parents and caregivers to manage smearing constructively. Being emotional or feeling that smearing is a demonstration of negativity from the individual can lead to inappropriate responses, such as punishment, which has been shown to be ineffective (Knell and Moore 1990; Piazza *et al.* 1998).

The overall aim of interventions with smearing is to minimize or, preferably, eliminate the behaviour. Smearing is a behaviour that can be addressed, regardless of how long it has existed in the individual or how often it has recurred. Strategies should form part of an individualized positive behaviour support (PBS) approach, so each strategy is tailored to individual needs and uses positive approaches, as outlined below. Importantly, parents and caregivers should liaise with school, other members of the family and any other people involved with the individual, so that they can all have a similar approach to smearing.

A note on strategies

In modern practice, aversion techniques are no longer considered appropriate means of managing behaviours such as faecal smearing (Addison 2013; Smith 1996). Aversive strategies include forcing a person to stand in front of or sit on the toilet for prolonged periods, often until urination or defecation in the toilet occurs. Additionally, punitive measures are not helpful in toilet training, because recent studies show that punishment-free or minimal-punishment training in toilet skills can lead to success in individuals with a 'wide range of abilities' (Rinald and Mirenda 2012, p. 934).

Only a few aspects of Azrin and Foxx's 'rapid toilet training' study are helpful 45 years on, such as their use of positive reinforcement and elimination schedules (diaries of urination), which continue to be used today and are described below (Azrin and Foxx 1971). Strategies that purport to offer rapid solutions to issues can compound the frustration some parents and caregivers may feel and lead to further annoyance and possible punishment for the individual involved. In addition, approaches that use punishment emphasize parents' and caregivers' power over individuals when for decades the disability movement and advocacy have developed to empower people with disabilities in modern Western society (Shakespeare 2013).

What to do when smearing occurs

Parents and caregivers should seek advice from a family doctor, with a view to a medical and/or psychiatric assessment. It is clear from research that individuals with intellectual and developmental disabilities and autism do not receive the same level of care and medical services as the general population, so parents and caregivers are in a key position to ensure individuals' needs are adequately addressed (Emerson and Baines 2010). A major difficulty may be helping the individual to understand any procedures which may take place so that he can co-operate with medical interventions using communication systems with which he is familiar. If individuals can't or won't allow doctors to examine them, it may be necessary as a last resort for the individual to have a general anaesthetic for a series of procedures to be performed in one episode, such as bloods taken, or any investigations.

Medical strategies could involve the following:

- Abdominal examination: palpating/feeling using the hands on the skin to look for lumps or hard areas and assess any pain or discomfort associated with the palpating.

- Abdominal X-rays may be taken to identify if there are loops of bowel distended with faeces and/or flatus, which indicate faecal impaction or obstipation (severe or complete constipation).

- Rectal examination: to work out the competence of the rectum (the length of colon leading to the anus), and assess if the rectum is constipated or has haemorrhoids.

- Perianal examination: visual and digital (using fingers) assessment of the area around the anus looking for obvious signs of infection or inflammation.

- Faecal examination: a specimen will be sent for laboratory assessment, looking for old (occult) blood which may indicate damage to the gastrointestinal system from possible chronic conditions such as ulcerative colitis, Crohn's disease or cancers.

Constipation

Research has shown that people with learning disabilities are less likely to have further medical investigations to uncover possible conditions (Heslop *et al.* 2013). Untreated constipation can cause additional complications such as haemorrhoids and rectal prolapse.

> Well, his bottom bleeds quite often but they just say, 'Oh, he's got a little tear.' A couple of years ago, the GP [identified] a little tear at the entrance and every now and then it pops... We have lactulose which we use if he starts to get constipated. When he's at home he's OK but what we'd find is when he went to respite he'd get constipated and that's been the pattern.
>
> Mother of 18-year-old young man with autism, cerebral palsy, Ehlers-Danlos syndrome, epilepsy, intellectual and developmental disabilities

Treatment of constipation consists of several strands. First, medical examination and investigations will demonstrate if constipation is present or if there is more extreme faecal impaction which requires hospital admission for interventions such as colonic washes, enemas and manual evacuation (the last of which may be what individuals are trying to achieve when they poke fingers into the anus and end up smearing).

NICE has produced guidelines which recommend Movicol as the medical intervention of choice in cases of constipation (NICE 2010). Prevention of constipation is ongoing with a goal of gaining a pain-free and soft stool. The strategies used include the following:

- Increasing the intake of fluids an individual drinks to around 1.5 litres per day (for children and young people), but not milk-based fluids, which potentially can increase the risk of constipation because they are a 'binding' fluid. The idea of drinking as much fluid as possible can be medically dangerous for people with seizures, kidney failure or certain other conditions.

- Increasing the amount of fibre in foods in the regular diet, such as fruit and vegetables and whole grains. If this is proving difficult, a dietitian could give advice.

- Using laxatives such as lactulose, or stool softeners such as docusate sodium, ideally in the short term. It is necessary for some individuals to take medication as part of their daily routine.

- Using enemas to ensure the colon (large intestine) is empty.

- Toilet training (see below) and monitoring bowel movements.

- Increasing physical activity if possible, since the muscle contractions in the abdomen, which occur particularly during walking, encourage bowel activity and movement of faeces along the colon.

It is important to point out that increasing fluids and dietary fibre alone may not alleviate constipation (Fleming and MacAlister 2016).

Medication, especially if given in high doses, can cause abdominal pain, nausea and lack of appetite until the dosage is correct and/or the constipation is resolved. It is thus important that any medication should be discussed with a doctor and the dosage given within guidelines. However, there is evidence that stool softeners and laxatives may not necessarily be effective for certain individuals (Matson and LoVulla 2009). Again, medical advice should be sought, the effects of any medical treatment should be monitored and parents and caregivers should seek more advice or another referral for specialist advice if necessary.

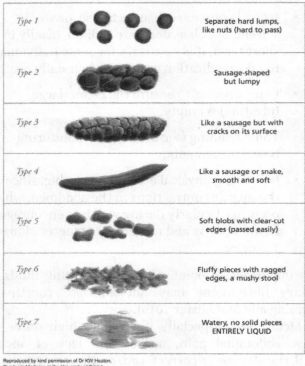

THE BRISTOL STOOL FORM SCALE

Type 1		Separate hard lumps, like nuts (hard to pass)
Type 2		Sausage-shaped but lumpy
Type 3		Like a sausage but with cracks on its surface
Type 4		Like a sausage or snake, smooth and soft
Type 5		Soft blobs with clear-cut edges (passed easily)
Type 6		Fluffy pieces with ragged edges, a mushy stool
Type 7		Watery, no solid pieces ENTIRELY LIQUID

Reproduced by kind permission of Dr KW Heaton, Reader in Medicine at the University of Bristol. ©2000 Produced by Norgine Pharmaceuticals Limited.

FIGURE 3.1 BRISTOL STOOL FORM SCALE

Rectal suppositories and enemas should be given strictly under medical direction and only as a last resort, particularly in children (Rubin and Dale 2006).

How parents and caregivers can give support
Monitoring how often individuals have their bowels opened is crucial to working out if constipation is an issue. The texture, colour and amount of faeces are important features to note in a diary to be presented to a medical practitioner. The Bristol Stool Form Scale gives clear images and descriptions of a continuum of stool formation from constipation to diarrhoea (see Figure 3.1). Using the scale as guidance will help parents and caregivers involved with the individual to give consistent reports of bowel movements to present to a doctor or other professional, or to keep for their records to support the individual.

Soiling may be a sign of constipation and should be noted in diaries. In addition, the individual should be helped to clean himself as quickly as possible to reduce the opportunity for discomfort and anal touching which may result. In addition, rapid cleaning ensures the anal area is less likely to become itchy and inflamed – although over-zealous cleaning may cause damage to the skin.

Encourage the individual to use the toilet after meals when bowels tend to move naturally. However, this should be ten minutes maximum, unless the individual is opening his bowels and needs longer to completely empty them. The scheduling of sitting on the toilet should not be for prolonged periods, which may make it more of a punishment than an encouragement. Do not expect a bowel movement (or, indeed, urination) every time the individual sits on the toilet.

Create a situation in which the individual can easily reach the toilet at home and at other locations. This does not mean sitting the individual outside a toilet for long periods, but ensuring, for example, that school will allow the individual to leave the class as needs be and that support staff in occupational settings are aware that the individual may need the toilet with little warning. The most basic way of communicating the need to use the toilet may be by the individual holding up or pointing to a card with a toilet on it.

Parents and caregivers should get into the habit of wearing plastic gloves when assisting individuals, regardless of whether they are dealing with faeces or not. This is important in the prevention of sexual abuse because the individual should understand that the ungloved hand is different and may indicate that inappropriate touch is happening (Reynolds 2013). For some individuals these kinds of differences may be their trigger to communicating that something is 'wrong' in their care and should form part of wider sexuality education about touch. If individuals have difficulty wiping their anus, disposable gloves may prevent faeces covering their hands and also will reinforce that the place for faeces is not on the skin.

Anal itching or *pruritus ani*

Anal itching is common and may be a diagnosis in itself. However, there usually is an underlying cause, which can be uncovered through careful medical history-taking, bowel diaries, physical examination (including the doctor putting a gloved finger into the anus) and tests. Common causes are skin conditions, infection, side-effects of medication, bowel disorders, other medical conditions and certain aggravating food and drinks.

The first step is to relieve the symptoms of inflammation and soreness by effectively cleaning and drying the anal area.

[Itching] that's another problem we have with him where the cerebral palsy (CP) comes in because his hips are very inverted it's really difficult to get him clean particularly if you're cleaning him standing up. And school and respite have a policy of not lying children down to clean them – it's a child protection thing, which I can see for girls but I don't get for boys because actually for boys cottaging happens from behind so I think for boys it's actually more appropriate to do it lying down than standing up. But they have these blanket rules, they cannot be laid down to be cleaned unless they're not able to stand. It's almost impossible to get him clean, if he's had a soft bowel movement, standing up. He comes home from school all dirty because he's not been properly cleaned because you can't get in to get that area properly cleaned.

Mother of 18-year-old young man with autism, cerebral palsy, Ehlers-Danlos syndrome, epilepsy, intellectual and developmental disabilities

Several things are important:

- Don't leave soap in the anal area; it won't keep the area fresh or clean. It will only irritate the anus further.

- Don't use bubble baths, perfumed soaps or talcum powder around the anus.

- Where possible, shower water into the anal area rather than rubbing with a cloth or sponge.

- Shower or bathe daily. This can become part of the individual's daily schedule. Of course, if the individual soils in between daily showers or baths, he should be helped to promptly clean the anal area.

- Instead of using toilet paper, which may chafe the area, use baby wipes or similar to clean the anal area. Remember that most wipes cannot be flushed down the toilet and should be bagged and placed in a main garbage bin.

- Anal moisture may continue between bowel movements if the individual is soiling, so the individual may need to clean himself or be cleaned in between using the toilet.

- Only put on underwear or nappies/diapers when the anal area is completely dry, otherwise you can seal in moisture which fosters infections and promotes itching and scratching.

- Minimize how hot the individual becomes at night by encouraging the use of a light duvet.

- Keep the individual's fingernails short to minimize possible damage to the skin through scratching.

- If underpants are worn (as opposed to nappies/ diapers), they should be relatively loose and changed on a daily basis, or more often if even slightly soiled.

- The individual should avoid tightly fitted clothing (see the section 'Restrictive clothing' below).

There are medications that reduce itching, notably local anaesthetics which can be bought in pharmacies, but it is important to get a medical opinion to ensure there is no underlying condition, such as haemorrhoids. However, the individual may have to wait for a medical consultation so the following treatments may reduce symptoms while waiting:

- Creams, gels and ointments are available to buy over the counter with a pharmacist's advice and should be applied thinly on the anal opening.

- If the individual can tolerate it, some medication comes with a small tube which can be gently eased into the anus, then the cream squeezed into the anal canal. The tubing can be lubricated with the cream. The individual should not be held down or forced to have the anus penetrated with the tubing, and the treatment must not be used as a punishment. Individuals may be extremely distressed if they have experienced anal rape, which may be the cause of the anal itching.

Unless anal itching is adequately treated, the behaviour may become part of an itch–scratch cycle, as shown in Figure 3.2.

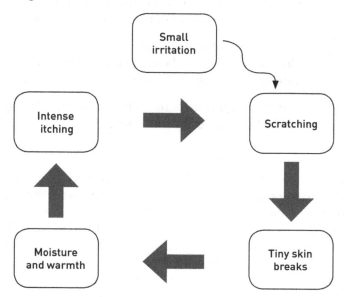

FIGURE 3.2 THE ITCH–SCRATCH CYCLE

While scratching, the individual may become interested in any faeces in the anal area and smear it to remove it from the fingers or for sensory reasons. Itching may become worse for women when urine or menstrual blood seeps onto the anus causing the individual to rub hard with toilet paper, further inflaming the anus.

Haemorrhoids (piles) and rectal prolapse

Medical investigations may include:

- talking to the individual, parents or caregivers to find out how the condition started, its symptoms, and the individual's medical history, such as chronic constipation

- testing a stool specimen for gastrointestinal infections

- visual examination of the anus, which may show a protruding mass of bowel or haemorrhoids

- barium enema and colonoscopy, when a special fluid and tubing is placed into the anus and up into the bowel to look for abnormalities

- other specialist tests to evaluate the functioning of the bowel, rectum and anus.

Strategies to support the individual

Parents and caregivers can help the individual prevent haemorrhoids or a prolapse becoming worse through dietary measures and increased fluid intake. Prevention of constipation is critically important to inhibit the individual from straining to pass faeces. If the person forces the stool out, this increases pressure in the abdomen and can cause haemorrhoids, and occasionally the rectum itself can be pushed out (or further out) of the anal opening (rectal prolapse).

See the previous section for strategies to limit damage to the anus and itching.

Dietary factors

There are foods and fluids that are known to cause irritation to the anal area, largely due to their acid content. However, foods and fluids that cause inflammation may vary from person to person. In addition, ready meals may contain 'hidden' foods that should be avoided, so it may be better to avoid these meals or scrutinize their contents carefully. Again, it is important to keep a diary of foods and fluids consumed and possible effects on the anal area to present to the medical consultant to assist in diagnosis.

> It's eased off now and in the last 24 hours he's had three [bowel movements]. He does swing very, very easily, less severe now than he used to be. He used to swing from diarrhoea into constipation, really, really easily just with a slight tweak to his diet or fluid intake. It's a bit more stable now. And we're better at managing that because his epilepsy's triggered by constipation so we have to be quite careful...but as he's hit mid- to late adolescence it has stabilized much more so we're down to between one and three a day.
>
> Mother of 18-year-old young man with autism, cerebral palsy, Ehlers-Danlos syndrome, epilepsy, intellectual and developmental disabilities

Infections

Antiparasitic, antiviral and antibiotic therapies may be prescribed by the doctor if there is an infection.

It is important to complete any prescribed courses of medication for them to be effective. Some doctors may be unused to adults with intellectual and developmental disabilities and may need encouraging to prescribe liquid medication. In addition, consultation with a dietitian may be necessary to determine whether a lactose-free diet is needed (often the case with crytosporidiosis), that the diet is as nutrient-intensive as possible and that the individual is ingesting enough fluids.

Dietitians can suggest alternatives or ways of improving the diet, even if only marginally, to help the individual develop broader food choices. In addition, supporting individuals at school or in supported living accommodation to eat meals provided by the establishment with other individuals can encourage a wider diet.

Genitourinary issues

Urinary tract infections are treated easily with antibiotics, although the tricky part may be obtaining a urine sample for testing if the doctor is cautious in prescribing and wants evidence of infection. Infections that are sexually transmitted should raise the possibility of sexual abuse taking place. Referral to the relevant authorities (social services in the UK, child protective services in the US and law enforcement) should be made as well as obtaining medical treatment at specialist facilities. However, this must be weighed against the possibility that the individual may be having consensual sexual activity, depending on the age and cognitive abilities of that individual.

For urinary incontinence to be adequately addressed, parents and caregivers should keep diaries for a minimum period of 48 hours (Neveus *et al.* 2006) showing:

- how much the individual urinates

- how often the individual urinates

- when the individual urinates, for example, time of day, when laughing, when stressed, at transitions

- if there are episodes of wet underwear, how often and how much.

Urine infections and urinary incontinence may contribute to or provoke smearing because they cause the perineal area to become damp and itchy.

Medical issues for ageing individuals

Menopausal women with intellectual disabilities and autism may benefit from the conventional treatment of hormone replacement therapy (HRT) and this should be considered earlier for women with Down syndrome due to early menopause (Schupf *et al.* 1997). This treatment can reduce the impact of lack of oestrogen, which can cause thin skin in the perineal area, leading to possible infection and inflammation.

Fibroids and other gynaecological problems need specialized medical input and may require surgery under a general anaesthetic. A diary of the individual's menstrual cycle (periods), noting how often they occur, for how long and if the blood contains clots, is essential to enabling the doctor to take an accurate medical history.

In men, prostate problems need specialized medical assessment and possible surgery. It is important to warn individuals that, in order to assess the size of the prostate gland, the doctor will have to insert a gloved finger into the individual's anus. A diary of how often the individual urinates, how much he passes, and if the urine looks like it has blood in it will help the medical practitioner.

Psychiatric conditions

Once the individual has been assessed by a psychiatric team using structured interviews and a review of medical history, a diagnosis can be made, then medication and therapies can be started. An important strategy is to support the family with family therapy and parent training and education about the diagnosed condition. It's worthwhile noting that many psychiatric conditions can exist alongside others (comorbidity), often because they share a genetic basis. For example, conduct disorder may coexist with clinical depression and/or ADHD.

Psychiatric/psychological strategies might include:

- Counselling therapy, such as cognitive behavioural therapy (CBT) for clinical depression and obsessive compulsive disorder.

- Mindfulness and relaxation techniques for conditions such as generalized anxiety disorder.

- Medication for individually diagnosed conditions, such as antidepressants for clinical depression and OCD. Practitioners should be wary of the antidepressant family of selective serotonin reuptake inhibitors (SSRIs), for example, sertraline or paroxetine, because noted side-effects are diarrhoea or constipation, both of which can precipitate smearing.

There is some debate as to whether or not psychotropic medications are effective against faecal smearing and other faeces-related behaviours (Powers 2005). Additionally, these drugs can cause or exacerbate constipation, which could lead to or worsen smearing behaviour. It is no longer considered acceptable practice to sedate individuals who are smearing or engaging in behaviours which challenge (Powers 2005).

Medications may be any of the following:

- Psychostimulants used to treat ADHD, such as atomoxetine, which have a major side-effect of constipation.

- Antidepressants such as imipramine and desipramine, although one of the most common side-effects is constipation.

- Selective serotonin reuptake inhibitors (SSRIs), for example fluoxetine and citalopram, which are used for clinical depression, OCD, post-traumatic stress disorder (experienced after sexual and other abuse) and panic disorder. A significant side-effect of SSRIs is diarrhoea or constipation.

- Antipsychotics, for example risperidone, are used to treat certain difficult behaviours, such as smearing, in individuals who have autism and other intellectual and developmental disabilities. However, there may be difficulties with sensitivities (see Chapter 4).

- Mood regulators, for example lithium, for mood disorders such as extremely low mood (clinical depression), often exaggerate the effects of antidepressants. They can cause diarrhoea, which should be monitored and diarized because it may cause worsening of smearing in individuals who already smear. In addition, diarrhoea may cause a recurrence of smearing or a very first episode of smearing.

Sensory factors

Perhaps one of the more difficult things parents and caregivers to understand is that children and adults who smear enjoy the experience in its own right. They enjoy the pungent smell of faeces, the texture and feel of it in their hands, the joy of spreading it around and the warmth of fresh faeces.

> He likes the smell because he likes strong, obscure smells. He really likes the smell because smell is very important to him. He will smell people and things when he meets them. And I think he likes the texture.
>
> Mother of 18-year-old young man with autism, cerebral palsy, Ehlers-Danlos syndrome, epilepsy, intellectual and developmental disabilities

These are all sensory experiences for the individual and understanding this may enable parents and caregivers to give less emotional responses to episodes of smearing, which has been shown to reduce smearing behaviours. In addition, the sensory benefits of smearing can be substituted in some circumstances.

> He's always loved that sort of sensory stuff, I just wonder if the smearing was 'Oh look, here's something soft and squidgy.'
>
> Mother of seven-year-old boy with Asperger syndrome and ADHD

Possible substitutes for faeces are:

- *touch:* warm play dough (just cooked), pudding, toothpaste, shower gel, cornflour and water mixture, clay and bread dough, sand and water mixture

- *visual:* finger painting, shaving cream, 'Slime', clay, bread dough

- *smell:* pungent-smelling cheese, Marmite, vinegar, essential oils, spices, scented lotions

- *sound:* texture will dictate sounds the material makes when squeezed.

Substitutions should be offered throughout the day so it becomes a routine, consistently implemented by all parents and caregivers involved with the individual. Having freely available substitutes where the individual usually smears, as well as scheduled substitutions, is more likely to reduce smearing. It may not work immediately, so trial and error may be necessary before a suitable substitute can be found.

Positive reinforcements for playing with substitutes should be swiftly implemented and be really motivational for that particular individual, although it may be better to avoid food reinforcements such as chocolate, which can become entrenched and potentially unhealthy. For any long-term change to take place, parents and caregivers need to be persistent and agree on a plan of action which can be applied at home and at school or in supported living communities. It can take months, if not years, to substitute a behaviour.

Emotional factors

Boredom may be a factor which is exacerbated at night when the house is quiet and there are no distractions. It can be helpful to provide the individual with a box of activities which are for night-time use and are in the bedroom. This might include play dough or faeces substitute (there is a recipe in Chapter 4) to mimic the faeces-related behaviours.

Individuals may also use smearing behaviour to remove themselves from situations or people they are uncomfortable with (Addison 2013).

Stress and anxiety may be extreme in some individuals, particularly those on the autism spectrum. Strategies depend on the individual. Those known to have a positive impact are:

- Concentration on and consistency in developing communication skills.

- Visual supports and aids, such as 'now, next, then' cards to show what is going to happen.

- Schedules and routines of daily activities or specific tasks, developed according to the individual's level of understanding.

- Alarms, which can enable some individuals to anticipate changes or other issues that cause them stress. This may be a basic clock alarm, a sand timer that lasts, say, ten minutes, or count downs by parents and caregivers from, say, ten minutes to five minutes, to two minutes before a change is going to happen such as moving from one activity to another.

- For some individuals, referral to a Community Child and Adolescent Mental Health Service (CAMHS) in the UK, or a psychiatric team to work with a psychologist or talking therapist where they can explore underlying issues and possible strategies to manage anxiety and distress.

If anxiety is adequately addressed, smearing behaviours may diminish without the need for other interventions (Fleming and MacAlister 2016).

Anger may be a result of extreme anxiety and fear of change or lack of understanding about what is happening or will happen to the individual. Much of this can be addressed with the strategies identified above.

The importance of teaching toilet skills

Many children with intellectual disabilities require additional support above that of typically developing children to gain toilet skills (Luiselli 1997), although it is still unclear exactly why some children with conditions such as autism struggle with gaining toilet skills and others with the same condition can attain such skills in line with their typically developing peers (Fleming and MacAlister 2016). Unless sufficient intervention is made available, poor toileting skills can continue into adulthood (Benninga 2004), when people with intellectual disabilities are less responsive to interventions (Ducker and Dekkers 1992).

However, it is never too late to support the individual to develop toilet skills, even if it is a slow process. One of the most important skills people with autism and intellectual and developmental disabilities need is toilet skills because:

- the more independent the individual is regarding toilet use, the less opportunity there is for the individual to be sexually abused (Reynolds 2013)

- the individual's self-esteem will be higher due to the accomplishment, which in itself leads to greater abilities to prevent all forms of abuse through assertion and ability to report abuse if it occurs

- smearing is likely to lessen as the individual is able to manage using the toilet.

> I think probably the biggest factor contributing to it [smearing] dying off is the fact that he's having the majority of his bowel movements in the toilet so there's much less opportunity for it.
>
> Mother of 18-year-old young man with autism, cerebral palsy, Ehlers-Danlos syndrome, epilepsy, intellectual and developmental disabilities

Creating a positive environment to promote toilet skills

- Drinks should be freely available to reduce the likelihood of constipation, enhance the sensation of bladder fullness and emptying, and reduce the possibility of urine infections.

- Opportunities to use the toilet should be freely available, which may need to include a stool for the individual's feet, a padded seat or grab rails. Any props that can enable the individual to manage on the toilet alone safely may maximize the ability of the individual to correctly use the toilet.

- There should be 'knocking' rules in the house/ school to prevent interruptions while using the toilet (Reynolds 2013).

- Ensure the toilet door is shut and, wherever safely possible, the individual is left alone to use the toilet.

- Allow time to use the toilet for defecating so that it is a relaxed experience with the least amount of stress as possible.

FIGURE 3.3 ENSURE PRIVACY IN THE BATHROOM

- Shutting the bathroom door and having a rule that people must knock will help the individual relax while using the toilet. Interruptions may cause the individual to become constipated through withholding faeces.

- Washing hands should be a routine after using the toilet. It shouldn't be a punishment for smearing (e.g. using very hot water or being rough).

Preparing for toilet training

- Whenever possible, change nappies/diapers in the toilet or bathroom. This may sound patronizing but we often change individuals in other rooms such as living rooms and bedrooms, for convenience or sometimes warmth. Individuals need to make the connection between urinating or defecating and the toilet room in the home.

> The toilet training was a very very very long and painful process... I don't know why we couldn't get him toilet trained, I think he couldn't be bothered, he'd just walk...around the garden and just poo as he walked. Then the more we tried to persuade him to toilet train, he'd just pull his trousers down and do it on the kitchen floor. So whether he didn't quite grasp I don't know. I don't feel that the smearing was necessarily connected with that but it was at the same time so it could have been.
>
> Mother of seven-year-old boy with
> Asperger syndrome and ADHD

- Whenever possible, change nappies/diapers with the individual standing. If appropriate to the individual's cognitive abilities, show him how and where to dispose of soiled nappies/diapers.

- Enable the individual to practise pulling his clothing up and down. This requires a level of physical development and can be practised when the child is dressing and undressing.

- Encourage the individual to put his faeces in the toilet. Individuals who are still wearing nappies/diapers can be taught to remove faeces from the nappy/diaper and put it in the trash. This is not a form of punishment but a way to enable our children to understand that the correct place for faeces is in the toilet.

- Encourage the individual to wipe his anus with toilet paper (which can be disposed of down the toilet with the urine/faeces) or wipes (which must be disposed of in the trash). It is important that the individual is clean when he has finished wiping, partly to prevent itchiness and also so that dirty underwear isn't interpreted as soiling. Wiping then looking at the paper or wipes to see if there is faeces on them, then repeating the wiping with new, clean toilet paper or wipes until the paper or wipes come back clean is a basic but important concept to teach.

- Get the individual accustomed to the sound of flushing, which can be a sensory challenge to some, as early as possible. The following strategies may help but the overall aim is to desensitize and therefore enable a level of independence:

  □ Avoid flushing the toilet when the individual is in the room.

  □ Warn the individual of when the toilet will be flushed.

  □ The individual could use ear defenders or plugs.

  □ Desensitize by introducing the sound at a distance (e.g. with the child downstairs while a toilet is flushed upstairs); THEN with the door open; THEN with the individual upstairs with the door opened as the toilet is flushed; THEN the individual can try being in the room with the door open as the toilet is being flushed; FINALLY the individual can be inside the room with the door closed.

□ Record the sound of the flushing of a toilet and introduce it quietly and with other sounds.

- Smells in the toilet may be disturbing to people with intellectual and developmental disabilities: not just human smells of faeces or urine but also the smell of strong cleaning fluids. It may help if individuals are involved in choosing air fresheners for the toilets and are allowed to spray the air after using the toilet if it is safe for them to do so. It is important to achieve adequate ventilation in toilets without the temperature of the room being too low and uncomfortable for the individual.

- Lighting in toilets can be too bright for some individuals. Using lower-wattage bulbs, coloured bulbs or night lights can help lower the light. However, some individuals like bright lighting because they fear darkness, so they may need high wattage and several lights on while they use the toilet.

- The ambience ('feel') of the room may not invite the individual to want to stay and use the toilet. This may seem trivial but is critical to enable the individual to relax and spend enough time to fully empty the bladder or bowels. The following are common issues for individuals with intellectual and developmental disabilities:

- ▫ Mirrors and bright or reflective tiling causing sensory overload and emotional outbursts.

- ▫ Uncomfortable temperature, preventing the individual from spending the necessary time to empty the bladder or bowel.

- ▫ Hard or cold toilet seat – use a padded or heated toilet seat.

- ▫ Fear of 'splash back' of toilet contents – place toilet paper on the surface of the water in the toilet before it is used.

- ▫ Perceiving toilet paper as scratchy – enable the individual to choose the toilet paper; use dampened or wet toilet paper for wiping, or use wipes.

- ▫ Fear of the size of the hole in the toilet – use a portable child's toilet seat.

- ▪ Practise washing and drying hands. Try to give the individual experiences of using and, therefore, listening to automatic hand driers so that he is more able to use public toilets. Try also to give the individual opportunities to use both hard and soft soaps. Introduce these as part of the daily routine. This can be helped by introducing schedules for what happens in the toilet, whether these are written lists or pictorial narratives.

- ▪ Find the right sort of motivation. For some individuals the notion that they will be 'like ordinary people' may be sufficient to promote their desire to gain toilet skills. For others, motivation may be achieved through rewards. Unfortunately, for many people with intellectual disabilities, their motivations may only be worked out through trial and error.

- There needs to be consistency across all people involved with the individual to promote continence and toilet skills. It may be possible to involve an individual with greater cognitive abilities in the process of working out a programme of toilet training, so he has an integral interest.

Steps towards using the toilet

Break down the process of using the toilet into bullet points or steps (see pages 84–90), which should be supported by pictures or symbols as necessary for each individual. Broken down, the complexity of learning to use the toilet independently is clear.

The process may be started by parents and caregivers giving the individuals opportunities to practise the steps, starting with sitting on the toilet without an expectation that there will be a 'result', which can put individuals under pressure. These opportunities should be scheduled and balanced so that the individual is not expected to spend all day sitting by a bathroom or having a constant stream of requests to sit on the toilet – and there should be no punishments should the individual soil or urinate himself.

Schedules might include sitting on the toilet for around ten minutes after eating a meal when the gastrointestinal system automatically starts to move. Sitting on the toilet should not exceed ten minutes unless the individual is still defecating. If the individual has some level of attention deficit disorder or ADHD it is important to limit the sitting times accordingly and to give immediate rewards for them to be effective.

Each step achieved can be reinforced by a reward system if that works for the individual. For many, having a sticker chart has no meaning, so other rewards may be necessary, including time playing with a special toy, time on the computer or a sweet or candy. These alternative rewards may be shown visually, perhaps offering the individual a choice of two rewards for achieving a step.

For others, rewards have little impact because they cannot control their soiling, perhaps because they are unaware of soiling, because they have overflow diarrhoea which they cannot hold in or because they have been abused and don't have the sensation that they need to open their bowels. They may be helped by medical treatment to alleviate and prevent constipation, or a long, slow process of counselling support and help to improve communication skills or learning to trust caregivers again and that abuse will not happen. The individual can then be reintroduced to toilet training. This is an important step which parents sometimes can feel is unproductive and that the individual simply cannot learn toileting skills because smearing behaviours have recurred. Ongoing support from professionals may be necessary for parents to use different strategies for toilet training.

> We've had nothing really [support]. We spoke to the school nurse... We have to put our names forward for the continence clinic but that's all... They talked about encouraging him to use the toilet and use the toilet more...but I think that'll take a lot longer than the lady thought... He'll stand and wee but he'll wee anywhere. If he goes in the shower I can guarantee that nine times out of ten as soon as he's in the shower he'll wee... We had a reward chart with superhero stickers and that worked really well for three or four weeks but not now.
> Father of four-year-old boy with autism and intellectual disabilities

Sometimes, as parents and caregivers, we can see the disabilities of our children rather than the abilities. By identifying separate steps towards independent toilet skills, parents and caregivers may be able to perceive how much the individual can manage and can visualize chipping away at the following step.

It may be helpful to pause at an agreed stage of toilet skills training so that they can be consolidated and the family or caregivers can 'rest' for a period. The important point is to pick up the toilet training again and not forget it among other demands (Fleming and MacAlister 2016).

The following steps guide the individual through the process of using the toilet.

STEP 1: FEELING THE NEED TO PASS FAECES
Identify this for the individual when he holds his abdomen with discomfort.

STEP 2: STOP DOING WHAT YOU ARE DOING
Some individuals do not want to leave the activity they are doing, so they may ignore the feelings of needing a bowel movement. Individuals with ADHD or a level of attention deficit may struggle to attend to toileting needs instead of their preferred activity. It may prevent confrontations and facilitate toilet training if the individual uses an alarm, such as a specialized wrist watch or an alarm clock, as a prompt to use the toilet.

STEP 3: MOVE INTO THE LAVATORY
The individual may need assistance to do this. See below for how to adapt the toilet for the individual.

FIGURE 3.4 FEELING THE NEED TO PASS FAECES

- It's important to teach the individual the link between the uncomfortable feelings in the abdomen and needing the toilet.

- It's possible to use visual schedules to show that the individual can return to what he is doing when he feels the need to go to the toilet. Otherwise the individual may withhold using the toilet and start to become constipated.

STEP 4: CLOSE THE DOOR

Privacy is an important aspect of the prevention of sexual abuse by reducing the opportunities for this to take place. Individuals need to understand that using the toilet is a *private* activity and, as parents and caregivers, we need to maximize individuals' independent ability to manage activities for which they would otherwise depend on others for support.

It is important that everyone in the house or supported living accommodation is aware that no-one is to interrupt the individual in the toilet. It is equally important that the toilet door closes/locks effectively.

STEP 5: PUT THE TOILET SEAT DOWN

The toilet seat may be too low, requiring a raised seat, or the individual may be scared of a large hole in the toilet bowl, so an 'inner' seat could be put in place.

STEP 6: PUT A 'STEP' IN FRONT OF THE TOILET

The individual's feet should be slightly raised above hip level, so it may be necessary to have a step to hand in the toilet.

STEP 7: PULL DOWN TROUSERS/PANTS AND UNDERWEAR

This requires physical ability and dexterity and can be practised.

FIGURE 3.5 ADAPTING THE TOILET EXPERIENCE

- To distract the individual from smearing or reaching into the toilet, have a box of toys which are only used in the bathroom or toilet.

- The individual's feet may need supporting with a foot stool so that his knees are above hip level.

- It may reassure the individual to have grab rails on the toilet and a padded seat.

- Massaging the abdomen may help the individual pass faeces.

STEP 8: SIT DOWN ON THE TOILET SEAT
AND PUT FEET ON THE STEP

To motivate the individual to remain on the toilet, provide special toys to play with or some other special interest items such as TV character magazines. These toys or items could remain for use in the bathroom or toilet only.

This may be particularly important if the individual has a level of attention deficit or ADHD where he moves quickly from one activity to another and finds it difficult to focus on one activity for any meaningful period of time. Furthermore, using the toilet may be a pretty poor option as an activity to these individuals compared with other things, so they need to be engaged with incentives and enabled to realize that they can return to a favoured activity after using the toilet.

STEP 9: PUSH THE FAECES OUT AND INTO THE TOILET BOWL

Some individuals find it difficult to focus on their abdominal muscles to push faeces out of the anus. By pretending to blow out candles on a cake, by blowing bubbles or blowing on a small wind instrument, individuals automatically apply pressure to the abdominal muscles. In turn, this helps the individual to feel the sensation of pushing and eases faeces out.

STEP 10: PULL X NUMBER OF SQUARES
OF TOILET PAPER OFF THE ROLL

Parents and caregivers who are able to leave the individual on the toilet often return to find most of a roll of toilet paper down the toilet, used or not. Teaching individuals to count a certain number of toilet paper squares or providing a limited amount of paper in individual piles for each wipe can enable them to contain their use of toilet paper.

FIGURE 3.6 WIPING CORRECTLY

It's important to teach individuals:

- to twist around to wipe the anus – practise this on a chair, turning side to side, perhaps reaching for a desired object

- to look at the toilet paper to see if there is faeces on it; this shows the individual that he is wiping the correct place and also when the anus is clean.

STEP 11: WIPE THE PENIS OR VAGINA AND DROP THE TOILET PAPER DOWN THE TOILET

Teaching individuals to wipe the 'front first' prevents infections being passed from the anus in faeces.

STEP 12: WIPE THE BOTTOM HOLE (ANUS) WITH PAPER AND DROP IT DOWN THE TOILET. REPEAT THIS UNTIL THERE IS NO FAECES ON THE TOILET PAPER.

It's important to teach individuals to look at the toilet paper after use so they can check when their anus is clean. This process can be taught using dolls or visual aids such as pictures, pictorial narratives or Social Stories™ (Gray 2010).

To teach the movements involved in wiping, the individual can practise by sitting on a seat and twisting around gently from side to side. It's important that the individual can twist either way so he can adapt to toilets where toilet paper is hanging on a different side, for example.

STEP 13: STAND UP FROM THE TOILET AND PULL UP UNDERWEAR AND TROUSERS/PANTS

STEP 14: FLUSH THE TOILET

STEP 15: WASH HANDS WITH SOAP AND WATER, THEN DRY HANDS ON A TOWEL

Try to desensitize your child to the noise of a hand drier and the harshness of paper towels, which are common in public toilets.

STEP 16: RETURN TO WHAT YOU WERE DOING

If our children understand that they can return to the activity they interrupted to use the toilet, they may be less likely to hold their bowel movements, which can lead to constipation.

Using a variety of toilets

People with intellectual disabilities and autism may find transferring skills from one situation to another challenging, including using toilet skills in different locations. Effectively they may only be 'toilet trained' in the home. Being unable to use toilets with which the individual is unfamiliar can cause significant difficulties. For example, children may be unable to go on residential school trips or respite. Constipation is more likely because the child may hold on to faeces to prevent the need to use an unfamiliar toilet. Additionally, urine infections may be more likely because children may drink less so that they don't need to use toilets other than the ones at home. Both constipation and urine infections are important causes of or contributors to smearing.

The following strategies may help:

- Start as early as possible to take children into public toilets to acclimatize them to the different environments. There are books written to inform individuals with intellectual disabilities and autism about public toilets (Reynolds 2014, 2015).

- Practise possible challenges at home, for example, helping the individual to use soaps and different toilet papers.

- Practise using hand rub and take this into public toilets in case there is no soap. Also take soft toilet paper and wipes to use as necessary.

- Take objects which may be familiar to the individual into toilets.

- Take a schedule developed and used at home, and use it consistently in public toilets. This is likely to be a list of steps in words and/or pictures. This may enable the individual to transfer toilet skills from home into skills for other toilets (Huntley and Smith 1999).

- Sensory issues may affect the individual's ability to use different toilets.

> She has to go into a disabled toilet because she can't deal with smells so we've got one of those Radar keys because she can't do with queueing or hearing people.
>
> Mother of eight-year-old girl with autism, epilepsy and intellectual and developmental disabilities

Using schedules to develop toilet skills

Regular visits to the toilet can be supported using a written and/or visual schedule to show what should happen in the toilet. Being prompted by a parent or caregiver may work for some individuals, but for others a timer, bleep on a watch or even alarm systems sewn into clothing (Lancioni *et al.* 2000) can be useful prompts, and this also relieves parents/caregivers of being the focus of annoyance when an individual has to leave an activity. For others, counting down the time until a scheduled toilet time can be more helpful.

The purpose of developing a schedule is to instil appropriate toileting skills and behaviours, and these should be reinforced with positive support, by ignoring incontinence and rewarding correct use of the toilet (Von Wendt *et al.* 1990). Some commentators suggest that individuals should be prompted to use the toilet immediately after a meal or at set times throughout the day. Others suggest prompting the individual to try having their bowels open before bedtime or after having a bath, which can be relaxing (Fleming and MacAlister 2016).

Some research suggests that such prompting does not give any advantage over the individual self-initiating use of the toilet (Ducker and Dekkers 1992). However, the individual may be unable to request the toilet through lack of communication skills or may have a lack of sensation telling him when the bladder or bowel is full.

Gravity helps faeces move down through the rectum and out of the anus so a period of undisturbed time on the toilet is essential.

Other strategies to support a toilet training programme

The following strategies can also be helpful:

- Reading stories which outline proper toilet behaviour (Reynolds 2014, 2015; Whelan Banks 2008).

- Watching videos about toilet skills. One study found that showing a child a toileting video three times per day enabled the child to gain a greater understanding of the purpose of using the toilet and appropriate toilet behaviours (Bainbridge and Smith Myles 1999).

- Social Stories™ (Gray 2010) or pictorial narratives tap into the visual abilities of many individuals with intellectual disabilities to gain insight into toilet skills and the fact that the correct place for faeces is down the toilet. However, they may not work with every individual.

> Everyone says to you, 'You need Social Stories™, write and draw a picture and that will make everything perfect.' A Social Story will not solve it! If I thought it would I'd have done it months ago. Re Social Stories, I just think that so many people think that draw it out and everything will be fine, it just seems to be the expert solution to everything, but every child is different and if it was that easy, I'd have done it. Like with the toilet training we had all the diagrams and the pictures... It still took four years to toilet train him.
>
> Mother of seven-year-old boy with autism and ADHD

- Having visual or listed toilet procedures in any toilet rooms in the home, ensuring that these are the same procedures as experienced and promoted at school.

- If the individual smears in the bath, this may be reduced by drawing up a bath schedule that gives rewards – anything that motivates the person – if the individual does not smear while bathing.

- Using massage on the individual's abdomen in the direction the bowel squeezes to encourage bowel movements. For individuals who have the cognitive and/or motor abilities to do so, parents and caregivers can teach them to rub their own abdomen with a view to being more independent.

- Individuals need to push and tense the abdominal muscles to empty the bowel and this can be promoted by teaching the individual to place a hand on the lower abdomen while blowing. This can be achieved by asking the child to pretend to blow out birthday candles or, if pretending is not within the understanding of the individual, he could blow a kazoo or similar toy for the same effect.

- Individuals can be taught relaxation techniques and deep breathing to alleviate sensory overload and anxiety.

A note about nappies/diapers

On the subject of nappies/diapers, their use can actually perpetuate a myth that the individual needs them (Ducker and Dekkers 1992). For example, if nappies/diapers are wet or soiled, parents and caregivers may surmise that the individual cannot manage without them, yet nappies/diapers may be preventing the individual from developing an ability to respond quickly enough to the sensation to go to the toilet. In addition, some individuals may not be aware that the correct place to urinate or have a bowel movement is the toilet because they have learned to only use nappies/diapers (Tarbox, Williams and Friman 2004).

It is important to stop using nappies/diapers if at all possible because they cause the anal area to become hot and sweaty or damp due to soiling, all of which can make the area itchy and may encourage smearing. In addition, toilet training will be hampered by use of nappies/diapers.

The following strategies may help withdraw the use of nappies/diapers:

- Always change nappies/diapers in the toilet or bathroom, so the individual starts to make the association between urination and bowel movements and the appropriate room.

- Parents and caregivers can gradually introduce the idea of not wearing nappies/diapers by helping the individual to sit on the toilet while wearing a nappy/diaper.

- When the individual shows signs of having their bowels open or urinating, such as grimacing or hiding behind the sofa, parents and caregivers can assist the individual to the toilet where he can crouch and urinate or defecate. Gradually the individual can be encouraged to sit on the toilet in a nappy/diaper while he urinates or defecates.

- Over time, the individual can have a hole cut in the nappy or diaper he's wearing so that urination or defecation can be quickly achieved sitting on the toilet as soon as there are signs of needing to go.

- Some individuals may want to hold a nappy/diaper as reassurance while they use the toilet, once they are at a stage of not needing to wear a nappy/diaper, such is the strength of the association between nappies/diapers and urination and defecation.

- It may take many months to get to the point where an individual can use the toilet without a nappy/diaper, so the process of learning or relearning is slow and gradual.

Functional behavioural analysis

Keeping diaries of smearing behaviours as they happen is key to working out what prompts the behaviour and what makes it persist. Once the possible causes of an individual's smearing are analysed through diarized information, it will be easier to address. In effect, all behaviours have meaning and purpose for the person doing them, which may be perceived as positive or negative for others. Smearing itself clearly has positives for the individual but many negative for others.

Behavioural approaches to smearing and other bowel-related unwanted behaviours have around 70 per cent effectiveness (Smith 1996). Functional behavioural analysis (FBA) is a formal way of addressing behaviour change and ensuring all involved in the support of the individual – at home, school or supported living – work together to improve the behaviour. Research shows that behavioural interventions using FBA are the most effective (Carr *et al.* 1999; Didden, Duker and Korzilius 1997; Scotti *et al.* 1991), and especially so for those with issues related to toileting skills (Beare, Severson and Brandt 2004; Bernard 1999; Carlson *et al.* 2008; Cascio *et al.* 2008; Sequeira and Hollins 2003).

Diaries

In busy homes with other children and possibly lack of sleep, keeping diaries may seem trivial or a luxury. However, these form the basis of the work to change the behaviour, so need to be vigilantly kept. In addition, diaries are useful tools to present to professionals or other caregivers involved in the individual's life. For example, a diary that notes if an individual is constipated can be extremely informative for a medical consultant to assess possible medical causes of smearing. A diary in which parents or caregivers have noted that smearing occurs after a change in diet may help a dietitian who is conducting an assessment.

Tracing bowel movements, noting size, colour and consistency, can help parents and caregivers work out an individual's pattern. This can demonstrate if the individual is becoming constipated, which usually happens over a period of time; it may seem to be a sudden change if parents and caregivers have not kept a record.

An important aspect of bowel care for individuals with intellectual and developmental disabilities is to ensure that those who still wear nappies/diapers are cleaned as soon as they have produced a stool. The perineal area can become itchy and even infected if it is not carefully cleaned, this in itself being a trigger for smearing. In other cases the individual may simply be exploring what is in the nappy/diaper or may realize that putting his fingers in the faeces will get the nappy/diaper changed quickly.

Diaries may help identify when an individual is likely to have his bowels opened, but this can be combined with the obvious signs that the individual is about to produce a stool, such as crouching, straining, sitting very still and a tense expression on the face. Sometimes the individual may move towards a quiet corner of a room or behind a sofa, for example. Prompt changing of nappies/diapers prevents the individual from having the opportunity to put his hands in faeces and start smearing.

Another important step towards tackling smearing is to try to ensure the individual's bowel is effectively emptied during the day. This may entail using medication and relying on diaries to monitor the amount and frequency of bowel opening.

Diaries will guide interventions or plans to eliminate or minimize smearing by generating ideas about the relationship between the individual's environment and smearing. The point of interventions is that they will be *positive*, with the explicit purpose of teaching the individual how to achieve what he wants using new, constructive ways. Diaries also provide ongoing data to monitor and possibly revise what interventions are taking place. Diaries should include the following information (ABC):

- A: antecedent – what happened *before* the smearing, including time of day, relation to food, events, where smearing took place, how much activity prior to smearing, who was there.

- B: behaviour – what actually happened, how extensive the smearing was.

- C: consequence – what happened directly *after* smearing, including the reactions of parents and caregivers.

This may seem obvious, especially if parents and caregivers have experienced smearing behaviours many times and feel as if they know the behaviour only too well. However, trying to study the behaviour as objectively as possible can enable parents and caregivers to 'see' prompts that they may not have recognized before. An example FBA smearing behaviour chart is shown in Figure 3.7.

Date and time	Antecedent What happens before the smearing? What's the situation?	Behaviour What exactly happens? What precisely does the individual do?	Consequence What happens after the smearing? What's your reaction?	Possible function of the behaviour What's the individual getting from smearing?
26/05/16 midnight.	Individual is in bed at night.	Individual smears faeces over the bedsheets and bedroom wall.	Parent becomes angry and tearful.	Individual is bored and no-one is around. Individual is constipated and faeces have seeped from his anus, causing itching and exploration of what has happened.

FIGURE 3.7 EXAMPLE FBA SMEARING BEHAVIOUR CHART

Schedules

Research into smearing (and eating) faeces has shown that altering schedules can reduce the behaviour. The individual should have changes in routine communicated to him in advance by whatever means he can understand.

One early study involved shifting the timing of an individual's shower to a point in the late afternoon/ early evening when smearing would take place and, crucially, allowed play in the shower. This eliminated the behaviours of smearing and eating faeces at that time of the day and reduced it at other times of the day (Friedin and Johnson 1979).

Another more recent study found that when a woman, who smeared as soon as she woke, was helped to the toilet immediately before her usual waking time, this was effective in eliminating the behaviour (Smith 1996).

Low-arousal response

Often smearing is a chronic behaviour so parents and caregivers have to manage it on a regular basis and can feel that there will be no end to scrubbing faeces off skin, clothes, furniture, and so on. The smell of faeces can pervade an entire house and parents and caregivers can feel that they themselves ooze the smell of faeces. The process of supporting and caring for someone who smears can be exhausting and even depressing. Parents may feel unable to ask for help because of embarrassment that this is how their child behaves, using what they may perceive to be a vile habit without any sense as to why it happens and what to do to tackle it. Being a parent and caregiver of an intellectually and developmentally disabled child can be isolating in itself, and smearing only adds to that level of loneliness.

One of the natural responses to finding an individual with faeces embedded in his fingernails, smeared throughout his hair and layered thickly on the wall and curtains is to feel anger and despair. Perhaps one of the most difficult aspects of smearing is trying to adapt our responses as parents and caregivers.

Some individuals who smear do so, at least in part, for the response of their parents and caregivers. They may feel an intense stimulus from having someone yelling and moving dramatically around the room and displaying despair in a way that gives sensory input to the individual. Explosive responses from parents and caregivers are attention, even if it is negative attention.

> He likes it if you get wound up with him, so he likes the fact that you'll then get cross with him, because that gives him feedback; he likes people to have emotional reactions. So a lot of his behaviour is emotion-fed, so again it's about trying to stay calm which is quite hard. So it's like a free toy really, I suppose, a freely available toy, which he does lots of things with: you can make shapes with it, you can put it all over the furniture, and then Mummy gets wound up about it.
> Mother of 18-year-old young man with autism, cerebral palsy, Ehlers-Danlos syndrome, epilepsy, intellectual and developmental disabilities

A low-arousal response involves being as emotionally neutral as possible when faced with an episode of smearing. This means neither a negative nor a positive reaction. Ways of doing this might be:

- Focus on your own breathing, in through the nose and out through the mouth, prior to starting to clear up.

- Use few, if any, words while clearing up following a smearing episode.

- Go somewhere alone for a few minutes to punch a cushion, use profanities if necessary, count to 20 or cry – whatever immediate emotional reaction you feel like making – but do it when the individual isn't there.

- Clean furnishings, flooring, beds, etc. of faeces away from the individual, so he cannot see or hear your responses to the ordeal of cleaning. Parents' and caregivers' emotions may reinforce the pain if smearing is an expression of distress due to forms of abuse, and may stop the individual expressing that hurt, even if inappropriately through smearing. Some parents on online forums suggest forcing individuals to clean up as a form of punishment or to somehow make them realize the impact of their behaviours. In practice, this may make the parents or caregivers feel better but there is no evidence that this reduces episodes of smearing, which is ultimately the aim of interventions. However, it is proven that a low-arousal approach can reduce, minimize or eliminate smearing (McDonnell, Waters and Jones 2002).

> Tried bribery, reward, praise, shouting and getting cross, withholding treats but nothing worked, so have lately just been cleaning him up and not really reacting. Then suddenly today he's done two [poos] in the loo – one first thing and one at lunchtime! Wow!
>
> Mother of seven-year-old boy with autism and ADHD

- When helping the individual clean himself, do so in silence or with the absolute minimum of interaction necessary to get the task done. Keep your face as neutral as possible. Low-key responses include behaving in a calm manner while helping the individual, so that your emotions don't seep out through your actions. For example, being rough in handling the individual or scrubbing him brusquely tells him about your emotions.

Demonstrating emotions by confronting the individual, acting out emotions through your behaviours or talking to others about smearing episodes in front of the individual may reinforce the behaviour by giving the individual (even though it's negative) attention. If the individual is using smearing for other reasons, such as to communicate previous experiences of abuse, then acting out or public discussion does nothing to address the real cause of smearing and serves to stigmatize the individual.

Positive reinforcement
The idea behind positive reinforcement is to give positive feedback to the individual for anything he is doing, aside from negative behaviours that you want to discourage. For example:

- 'That's great sharing with your sister.'

- 'Good trying [to feed yourself].'

By flooding individuals with praise during their daily living, they will gain attention without having to smear for attention, even if it's negative attention. This is not to imply that parents and caregivers cannot have some negative responses to unwanted things the individual does; after all we are human. However, making these minimal while highlighting the positives is shown to reduce behaviours we want to stop.

Rewarding desired behaviour

Some children have the cognitive abilities to understand rewards for appropriate behaviour. Reward charts are a way of formally and visually encouraging individuals to behave in acceptable ways for desired rewards. Desired behaviours may be any of the following:

- faeces in the toilet or in the nappy/diaper and nowhere else (i.e. not smearing)
- fingers and hands are clean (i.e. not 'digging' at the anus)
- nappies/diapers intact (i.e. not picking at nappies/diapers)
- nappies/diapers untouched (i.e. not dipping fingers into faeces in nappies/diapers)
- faeces left untouched in the toilet bowl (i.e. not picking faeces out of the toilet bowl).

Be wary of rewarding something over which the individual may have no control. For example, avoid rewarding clean underwear – that is, not soiling – if the child may not be able to prevent soiling. Rewards themselves should be immediate and have significance for the individual. Additionally, large rewards, such as seeing a movie at the cinema, could be given after a period of time when the individual has behaved in the desired way, for example, after a week of no smearing, with small, immediate rewards building up to the large one. Examples of rewards are:

- praise, high fives, hugs
- drawing paper

- time painting pictures
- computer games
- a movie
- sweets/candy or chocolate
- a new toy car
- a magazine
- stickers.

One of the keys is not to focus just on food rewards if possible. However, I have met parents whose children are solely motivated by sweets/chocolate, in which case limit the quantity of sweets in any reward. Rewards must be of value to the individual, without being critically important. For example, if an indinvidual carries toy cars in each hand for security, it would not be constructive to remove the cars to return them later as 'rewards'. Finally, rewards should be positive rather than something that could be construed as a punishment. For example, giving a piece of candy may be a reward but withholding candy should not be perceived as a punishment by parents and caregivers.

Many children, for example those with ADHD, find the concept of waiting for rewards challenging, so their rewards have to be immediate to be effective. This means that using larger rewards may be less understood, unless small rewards build up to large rewards; for example, being rewarded with small coins in a jar, leading to being able to buy something large with the coins when the jar is full.

Inadvertent rewards

Sometimes parents and caregivers can unwittingly give a reward for smearing. For example, it may be tempting to place your child in front of the television or give him computer games to keep him occupied and focused while you clean up faeces from a smearing episode. Similarly, running a bubble bath for the child may seem to be the right action, if for no other reason than to soak faeces from under his fingernails and replace the offensive smell of faeces with a more pleasant fragrance. However, in both these examples, parents and caregivers are effectively 'rewarding' the smearing because they are giving a pleasant experience as a direct result of a smearing episode. This reinforces an unwanted behaviour which encourages repetition of smearing.

Instead of these two inadvertent rewards, parents and caregivers could give a quick shower, efficient wash and few words as opposed to a bubble bath, or a book could be given to occupy the individual rather than a screen activity.

Supporting the individual with hygiene

Remember that having individuals clean themselves should never be regarded as a punishment. They may need considerable help, and withdrawing the necessary support can be regarded as a punitive behaviour by parents and caregivers. Instead, individuals should be supported to the level they need to safely and competently manage to clean faeces off themselves. Wipes, clean clothing and plastic bags for soiled clothing should be readily available to help the individual in self-cleaning.

Consequences

Some individuals may understand the notion of actions leading to consequences. For these people, a picture narrative, visual schedule or even verbal discussion may enable them to recognize what would happen as a result of their actions, such as smearing.

Addressing sexual causes

There are three distinct areas in which smearing may have a sexual cause: first, as part of a solo sexual act; second, as a response to sexual abuse; and third, to prevent sexual abuse and violence.

Solo sexual act

The anus has many nerve endings, and it can be sexually arousing when they are stimulated by fingers, or objects such as vibrators. Depending on the level of independence of individuals, they may use household objects to elicit sexual excitement. The purpose of becoming sexually aroused in the presence of faeces may be to use soft stools as a lubricant (Case and Konstantareas 2011; personal communication 2015). In addressing smearing as part of a sexual act, parents and caregivers may give water-based lubricant to replace faeces as a lubricant in masturbation.

In addition, individuals need time alone ('private time') in their bedrooms where they will be undisturbed for a lengthy amount of time to be able to reach a sexual climax. It is suggested that time for masturbation is scheduled into an individual's day when nappies/diapers can be removed to allow access to the genital area (Reynolds 2013).

Sexuality education should be a process over a period of time from childhood onwards in preparation for puberty, and should include touch, public and private behaviours, personal space and body changes as basics. Within this the issue of masturbation and lubrication should be discussed through whatever means of communication the individual uses, whether by words (Hartman 2013), visuals (Hartman 2015a, 2015b), picture narratives (Reynolds 2014, 2015) or symbols (Makaton Charity 2008).

Sexual abuse

Excessive masturbation, resisting help to change nappies/diapers or use the toilet, bedwetting, faecal and urinary incontinence and soiled underpants may all be signs of sexual abuse. There are many other signs or symptoms but these are specific to the focus of smearing.

There are two other key ways in which sexual (and other) abuse is significant to smearing behaviour.

First, faecal smearing has been categorized as a form of post-traumatic stress when its cause is sexual and possibly physical and emotional abuse or child sexual exploitation. Historically there was a myth that individuals with intellectual and developmental disabilities could or would not be sexually abused and a belief that they would not respond to counselling therapies conventionally used to support typically developing children/adults. We now know these to be fallacies, and individuals with intellectual and developmental disabilities should be referred for specialist psychological assessment and counselling. However, these historical beliefs are reflected in notable gaps in service provision in the UK and the US and fewer interventions for disabled children as opposed to non-disabled children who have been sexually abused (Cooke and Standen 2002; Lightfoot and LaLiberte 2006).

Second, smearing may be used to repulse a sexual abuser so that the abusive behaviour stops. The obvious repulsion of an abuser is reassuring for the individual and will promote the continuance of smearing, which acts as a protective barrier and therefore is a positive thing for the individual (personal communication).

Specifically it is crucial for parents and caregivers not to demonstrate their emotions, such as disgust or anger when clearing up, because this may reinforce the deep trauma felt by the survivor of the abuse. Smearing in this circumstance is not an aggressive or defiant behaviour but a means of expressing deep distress which he cannot express in other ways. Strategies that may support the individual could involve:

- continuing to develop communication skills to try to help the individual start to express his upset at his pace

- seeking professional support rather than directly asking the individual why he smears; if the individual could explain in words or communicate why he smears, he would not need to smear in the first place

- low-arousal responses

- positive responses and consistent support for the individual which over time may increase his self-esteem and feeling of security.

Restrictive clothing

Restrictive clothing is modified clothing that is a form of mechanical restraint in that it prevents individuals from reaching into the clothing to investigate their anal area (Hayward 2010). These clothes tend to cover the entire body with no access at the front, sometimes achieved by wearing the item back-to-front. Sometimes they are fitted, stretchy fabric such as Lycra™ or Spandex™, or non-breathable fabrics such as rubber wetsuits. Restrictive clothing may consist of any of the following:

- jumpsuits

- bodysuits

- overalls

- onesies

- Lycra™ garments such as leotards, swimming costumes and cycling shorts

- 'dementia suits' – specifically designed to prevent undressing and access to private body parts.

In addition, many parents and caregivers go to extreme lengths to make attire for individuals who smear, for example by sewing or pinning together fitted (often sleeveless) T-shirts and underwear or fitted jogging bottoms or leggings. Online forums are full of advice about using copious amounts of duct tape to seal in nappies/diapers, and to provide a seal around sleeves and even necklines. Fabric hook and loop fasteners (e.g. Velcro™) are also suggested as a means of sealing the individual into clothing.

Advantages of restrictive clothing:

- It allows a few extra minutes for parents and caregivers to respond appropriately.

- It may temporarily reduce the level of stress on parents and caregivers.

- Schools may use a level of restrictive clothing so they are able to concentrate on other issues, such as focusing on other children, if there are not enough support staff.

- The itch–scratch cycle associated with *pruritus ani* (itchy anus) may be broken if there is a period of no scratching whatsoever. However, this must be weighed against the fact that heat (which is increased in restrictive clothing) significantly worsens the itching.

Disadvantages of restrictive clothing:

- It makes independent toileting or opportunities to practise toilet skills impossible because of lack of freedom of movement, inability to remove the necessary attire to use the toilet and accompanying assumptions that the individual cannot learn toilet skills (Carroll and Kincade 2007).

- For individuals who have limited motor skills, restrictive clothing may prevent further development of motor skills by limiting their movements. Alongside this, accidents from falling over and other difficulties may arise, such as being unable to roll over in bed or getting 'stuck' in one position in bed.

- Some restrictive clothing binds or covers the individuals' hands to prevent them reaching into their underwear or nappy/diaper. Again, this directly inhibits the person's development of manual dexterity and manual manipulation of objects, which is achieved through practice.

- It may prevent parents and caregivers seeking a permanent resolution to smearing, because they mistakenly believe that restrictive clothing is the solution. Restrictive clothing therefore can become used indefinitely.

- The heat generated in such clothing can exacerbate medical conditions, causing further skin irritation in the perianal area and general discomfort that may cause sleep disturbances. It also has been reported to cause dehydration (Rennie *et al.* 2000). In consequence, this may lead to fatigue and exhaustion.

- Duct tape and Velcro™ fastenings can directly injure skin, especially if used repeatedly, leaving skin open to infections and causing discomfort to the individual (Stancliff 1999), while stretchy fabric has been associated with friction sores on the skin (Nicholson *et al.* 2001).

- Using this clothing sets up a scenario with parents and caregivers versus individuals, possibly fostering a confrontational relationship.

- Research shows that applying restrictive clothing without it being in the context of unwanted behaviour can have damaging effects on the psychological and social development of the individual (Rojahn, Schroeder and Mulick 1980). In other words, permanently clothing the individual in this way means that the individual is being constantly physically restrained without making the connection with his smearing behaviour.

- Restrictive clothing also has been shown to decrease positive behaviours of individuals with intellectual/developmental disabilities, such as social interaction and willingness to be involved in play (Hayward 2010).

- Studies show that such clothing influences the responses of others, who make negative assumptions about the individual's intelligence and potential (Nisbett and Johnson 1992).

- Smearing may result in adverse responses from parents and caregivers, which may be reinforced by permanent restrictive clothing. Parents and caregivers may thus express less positive attention and reinforcement towards individuals (Hayward 2010).

- Research also has demonstrated that stereotyped movements of individuals may increase as a direct effect of restrictive clothing (Hayward 2010).

- Use of restrictive clothing contravenes the thrust of modern support for people with disabilities in Western society, which is based on human rights and dignity, both of which are undermined by the practice of clothing individuals in garments that restrict movement (Shakespeare 2013).

- Restrictive clothing can identify an individual as being disabled and can be integrally disempowering. However, the opposite also is true, so parents and caregivers can support self-esteem and personal development of the individual by enabling him to dress in garments that do not earmark him as disabled.

- Restrictive clothing can be difficult to put on, especially stretchy fabric products or wetsuits. This has several impacts, including possible friction burns or damage to the skin, and forcing limbs into clothing causing injury to the individual. In turn this may lead to aggression from the individual, who may be hurt or uncomfortable.

- In turn parents and caregivers may be under more physical strain due to the impact of trying to dress individuals in restrictive clothing. If the individual needs to be helped to change a nappy/diaper, the process is far more onerous if restrictive clothing has to be removed and replaced (Nevala *et al.* 2003).

- If these types of restrictive clothing are too tight, they can cause restriction of blood flow to the peripheries, that is, the fingers and toes (Rennie *et al.* 2000).

Conclusions about restrictive clothing

The use of restrictive clothing should be viewed as supporting behavioural interventions, whose ultimate goal is to teach the individual toilet skills. Wearing such clothing thus is a temporary measure, put in place to try to achieve specific objectives. It should not be regarded as a panacea for smearing.

Restrictive clothing should be reviewed as part of the individual's support and care plan and not assumed to be permanent. Reviews should aim to gradually reduce the amount of time when restrictive clothing is used. For example, if restrictive clothing has been used continuously, parents and caregivers could unfasten the clothing for a given period every hour and slowly increase the time.

EASY-READ SUMMARY

The first step in managing smearing is to take the person to a doctor to see if there is a physical or a mental health problem causing the smearing. The person may need tests to work out what's wrong. Punishments should not be used to try to stop or reduce smearing. Instead, parents and caregivers should do positive things, such as making sure the person eats more fibre and drinks more, and should keep a diary to show when the person passes faeces and what the faeces are like.

Other things parents and caregivers can do are to help the person keep his bottom hole clean and dry and try to stop the person wearing nappies/diapers. The author of this book does not think clothing that stops the person reaching his bottom hole, like onesies, is a good idea. Instead, the most important thing is to teach the person how to use the toilet.

If the person has been attacked sexually, he should be helped by professionals, such as counsellors.

Parents and caregivers can best help the person by not reacting to smearing, but by being calm, and also by trying to say good things when the person is doing good things, like eating or playing well.

The pictures in the chapter

Constipation is often a problem that causes smearing. Sometimes the person can poo their underwear when they are constipated. The aim is for poos to be like Type 4 on the Bristol Stool Form Scale (Figure 3.1). You can use this picture to write down or show a doctor what type of poos the person is having, which can assist treatment.

The picture of the itch-scratch cycle shows that itchy bottom holes can get worse and worse unless you clean the bottom hole quickly with simple soap that has no smell. The bottom hole should be washed and dried thoroughly and gently. You should make sure that no toilet paper is rubbed in. Wee or blood from a period can leak near the bottom hole and can also make itching worse.

Figure 3.7 shows you how to work out why the person is smearing by seeing what happens **before** the smearing, how and what the person smears and what happens **after** the smearing. If you write this down, it could help the doctor treat the person and help stop the smearing.

The other pictures in the chapter illustrate important steps that should be taken during toilet training.

4

Eating Faeces

Definitions

Eating faeces is clinically called coprophagia. Parents and caregivers may discover individuals ingesting their own faeces or pulling another's faeces from the toilet or from the nappy/diaper of a sibling, for example. Parents and caregivers understand the person-intensive nature of trying to prevent an individual eating faeces, often describing how they cannot leave the individual alone for fear of an opportunistic episode.

Ingesting faeces is widely considered to be a form of pica, which involves eating objects that are non-nutritive (not nourishing to the body) (Motta and Basile 1998). Pica might include stones, cigarette butts, paper, cardboard, plastics, washing powders, cleaning fluids and items of clothing (Matson *et al.* 2011). Both children and adults can indulge in pica, sometimes focusing on one object, sometimes on many different inedible objects. Ingesting faeces may take place alongside eating other objects not designed to be eaten.

Other behaviours commonly associated with eating faeces are:

- faecal smearing
- eating objects other than faeces
- hypersexuality
- aggression.

(Josephs *et al.* 2016)

However, some of these other behaviours may be a way of responding to physical illness when the individual cannot explain that she is feeling unwell.

How common is it?

Eating faeces is largely associated with children and adults with intellectual and developmental disabilities (Parry-Jones and Parry-Jones 1992). In one study ingesting faeces was found in a case of so-called high-functioning autism (autism without intellectual disabilities), which the authors believed was the first recorded case of this sort (Pardini and Guida 2010).

Research has shown that anything between 4 and 26 per cent of children and adults with intellectual disabilities engage in pica in general (Dudley, Ahlgrim-Delzell and Calhoun 1999; Matson *et al.* 2011). Among these, pica occurs more in women than men and appears to decrease with age (Rose, Porcerelli and Neale 2000).

The greater the additional needs and the lower the cognitive abilities of the child/adult with intellectual and developmental disabilities, the increased likelihood there is of pica behaviours (Ali 2001). One study found it is more commonly practised in people on the autism spectrum than those with Down syndrome (Kinnell 1985). This may be because pica may be part of OCD which is closely linked with autism (Russell *et al.* 2005), although some commentators believe that pica is a condition in its own right, not part of any other impairment (Matson *et al.* 2011). Clearly this is a subject that needs more research.

Before the age of two years, eating faeces and pica of other objects in typically developing children is within what is considered 'normal' behaviour (Barltrop 1966). Beyond this age, eating faeces may indicate an underlying medical, psychiatric or behavioural condition. The latest *DSM-5* has revised the criteria for pica so it is now classified as an eating disorder and can be applied to people of any age; it is defined as the ingestion of non-nutritive objects for at least one month (APA 2014).

The incidence of ingesting faeces is unclear. This may be partly due to lack of research in this area of medicine, leading to a lack of real understanding and clear evidence for medical treatment (Pardini and Guida 2010). Additionally, parents may be reluctant to seek medical or other support, due to embarrassment and shame and, perhaps, a belief that only their child eats faeces.

A note about strategies

Perhaps because of a lack of research in this area, the information which does exist still refers to strategies used anything from 26 to 45 years ago (Azrin and Foxx 1971; Mackenzie-Keating and McDonald 1990). Although these data have produced anecdotal evidence of 'success' in limiting or stopping eating faeces in the short term, the methods used are not evidence-based, have poor experimental control and are not acceptable today (Ing, Roane and Veenstra 2011).

Over-correction, when the individual might be made to clean the bathroom or stand facing a wall (Foxx and Martin 1975), and aversion methods involving spraying individuals with water or other means of causing discomfort (Challenging Behaviour Foundation 2013) have been surpassed by positive behaviour strategies.

Some parents and caregivers advocate using mouth appliances, which are a form of physical constraint and risk injuring the individual's mouth and teeth. Intrusive interventions such as mechanical restraints and blanket use of psychotropic drugs are not recommended as part of modern support of people with autism, intellectual and developmental disabilities and, as well as having numerous unwanted effects, have not proven to be effective (Matson *et al.* 2011).

Punitive measures in cases where people eat faeces have been shown to increase the individual's aggression and frustration, both of which may be avoided with different approaches (Hagopian and Adelinis 2001). However, non-aversive or non-punitive techniques have been demonstrated to alter behaviours and do so over the long term (Ing *et al.* 2011); these will be described below.

What are the risks of pica?

Pica may result in intestinal obstruction or more immediate effects of choking, vomiting, poisoning and constipation, depending on the objects ingested. Surgery may be necessary to remove solid objects from the gastrointestinal tract or repair damaged tissue.

Ingesting faeces can also have physical effects, notably infections. These may include intestinal parasites and blood-borne pathogens (Parry-Jones and Parry-Jones 1992), such as Shigella, hepatitis A and hepatitis E (Pardini and Guida 2010). Short term, eating faeces can cause diarrhoea, lack of appetite, weight loss, nausea and vomiting. The individual may feel unwell and be unable to communicate this to parents and caregivers.

In addition, eating faeces can be associated with oral infections including inflammation and infection of salivary glands in the mouth (Donnellan and Playfer

1999). Antibiotics will treat infections, but if not treated promptly, there may be further physical complications.

Regular oral hygiene helps to prevent mouth infections, but should not be regarded as a form of punishment, for example, by using soaps or other inappropriate cleansing materials if eating faeces occurs. Rough treatment of the mouth can make it more vulnerable to infection and there is no evidence to show that this prevents the individual eating faeces in the future.

Possible reasons for ingesting faeces

- Pica can be linked to a lack of minerals in the diet, particularly zinc and iron (Edwards 1959). Pregnant women have been documented as engaging in pica when they have dietary deficits. Research into animals, notably dogs, ingesting faeces reveals that they, too, may be seeking elements that are missing from diets.

- Social responses to the individual eating faeces may reinforce the behaviour, whether the attention gained is positive or negative. For example, demonstrations of emotions in body language or verbally may stimulate the individual and give her sensory feedback which she may want to experience again by repeating the behaviour.

- Ingesting faeces is such a social taboo that it may be precisely the behaviour to achieve feedback, which may address other emotional needs such as relieving boredom or frustration.

- Sensory issues may cause individuals to consume faeces, which have a distinctive, intense smell and taste. Eating faeces may be combined with smearing, which may heighten the sensory experience of the individual. Individuals who engage in pica often choose distinctive and unusual-tasting objects such as cigarette butts and faeces.

- Sometimes a lack of communication skills may prevent an individual from requesting something, whether this is an object such as a favourite toy, an activity such as a computer game or even food or drink. If the individual receives the desired object as a result of ingesting faeces, this will promote a repetition of the behaviour to achieve the same result.

- Some research has found that individuals eat faeces either to be removed from a situation they dislike or to avoid doing something they dislike (Addison 2013). Largely, if an individual ingests faeces, the behaviour will become the focus of attention and the individual is likely to be removed from the unwanted activity or place while the immediate issue becomes cleaning teeth, tongue, fingers, and so on. The 'success' of ingesting faeces for the individual may ensure that the behaviour is repeated because she gains something positive.

- Tasting and eating faeces may result from an episode of self-exploration, which itself may be caused by irritation of the anus (as with smearing), boredom or an attempt to masturbate as part of social/sexual development.

- Studies have shown that pica is associated with mental health issues (Decker 1993).

Medical assessment

Blood tests can detect below-normal levels of important minerals such as zinc, which is an essential trace element needed for the immune system to work properly and is vital for the sense of smell and taste. It is found in dark meat, nuts, whole grains, beans/peas and yeast.

Low zinc levels affect the gastrointestinal, central nervous, immune, skeletal and reproductive systems (Roohani *et al.* 2013). It causes a range of symptoms such as loss of appetite, diarrhoea, weight loss, mental fatigue, poor wound healing, impotence and, notably when we consider ingestion of faeces, taste abnormalities including poor sense of taste (Dharmarajan, Gunturu and Pitchumoni 2012). However, many of these signs of illness are general and communication difficulties and level of cognitive abilities may complicate matters, so careful medical examination and assessment are necessary. Low zinc levels may be caused by:

- lack of zinc in the diet

- conditions causing malabsorption of food, such as intestinal and bowel disease

- increased excretion of zinc due to biliary or gastric conditions which prevent the reabsorption of zinc into the body (Roohani *et al.* 2013)

- increased need for zinc: for example, there is evidence that people with Down syndrome have low levels of zinc which may impair their cognitive functions (Eastland 2001); in addition, children, adolescents and pregnant women require more zinc.

Low levels of iron (anaemia) can be identified in an individual's blood. Iron is needed to make the protein haemoglobin which carries oxygen around the body. Anaemia can make the person appear pale and feel breathless, fatigued and dizzy. Foods containing iron are meats, beans and seeds, green vegetables such as spinach, dried fruits, eggs, seafoods and breakfast cereals fortified with iron. Anaemia can be caused by:

- Heavy menstruation in women, which can affect all females regardless of intellectual/developmental disability. Periods may be heavier for the first year after a young woman starts periods or when an older woman is going through the menopause. Other causes of heavy periods may be fibroids, endometriosis, infections or cancer of the womb. In addition, some forms of contraception can cause heavier periods, such as intrauterine contraceptive devices (commonly called the 'coil'), injected contraception such as Depo-Provera, and (for at least the first year after implantation) contraceptive implants. These forms of contraception can be favoured by women with autism, intellectual and developmental disabilities or their advisors because they do not require the individual to remember to regularly take medication.

- Too little iron in the diet, which can be an issue for children with autism, whose diets may be self-restricted to a few items.

- Sometimes children undergoing a growth spurt may become anaemic due to the added demands for oxygen by the growing body.

It is important to have medical investigation into possible consequences of eating faeces, such as infections and parasites. Interventions might include:

- laboratory tests on faeces, blood, urine and/or phlegm specimens

- abdominal X-rays

- colonoscopy (a tube with a tiny camera in it to observe bowel walls and take biopsies if necessary)

- CT scan – a series of special X-rays (this should not be confused with an MRI scan, which involves lying in what looks like a tube).

Mental health issues

Psychiatric assessment should be conducted after physical conditions have been excluded as the cause and the individual's toilet skills and abilities have been assessed to work out if a psychiatric condition contributes to ingesting faeces, possibly through lack of understanding that the place for faeces is in the toilet or, if necessary, in a nappy/diaper (Pardini and Guida 2010).

Although getting a clear psychiatric diagnosis is notoriously difficult to achieve among people with developmental and intellectual disabilities (personal communication), identifying conditions which may underlie the ingestion of faeces, such as severe anxiety disorder, and OCD, which is often associated with autism (Russell et al. 2005), can direct psychiatric support and treatment. It has been suggested for decades that pica and other 'eating disorders' such as ingesting faeces are associated with psychiatric conditions (McLoughlin 1987), particularly clinical depression (O'Brien and Whitehouse 1990).

Other research reiterated a link between treating an individual with antidepressants and a concurrent reduction in pica as the individual recovered from clinical depression, suggesting that pica, eating faeces and other so-called 'challenging behaviours' may be linked to depression (Jawed *et al.* 1993). Antidepressants such as serotonin, long-standing antipsychotics such as haloperidol (Josephs *et al.* 2016) and atypical antipsychotics like perospirone (Beck and Frohberg 2005) have also shown positive results. However, these may be less appropriate in individuals on the autism spectrum who tend to have a higher incidence of hypersensitivity and side-effects from medications (Pardini and Guida 2010).

In pronounced cases, individuals may need to be given inpatient hospital treatment for assessment and treatment prior to discharge into their home in the community. Some medications, such as newer antipsychotic drugs like aripiprazole, have been shown to have positive effects on ingestion of faeces in people with autism spectrum conditions (Pardini and Guida 2010) although this may not be lasting (Haoui, Gautie and Puisset 2003).

During times of distress or anxiety, pica and eating faeces may become worse, which could imply that the individual has a mood disorder, such as bipolar disorder, which is cyclical and involves periods of depressive moods (Jawed *et al.* 1993). For parents and caregivers the implication is that strategies need to be in place to communicate to the individual about changes in her routines or to help her understand what is happening in her day. Modern methods of visual communication by using 'now, next, then' cards and pictures to show what to expect, visual schedules and Social Stories™ (Gray 2010) all support the individual's understanding.

Functional behavioural analysis

Research using FBA has shown that it is possible to significantly reduce or eliminate ingestion of faeces (Ing *et al.* 2011; Piazza *et al.* 1998; Roane *et al.* 2003). FBA will help parents and caregivers form a plan to minimize or eliminate the behaviour, using the strategies outlined below, depending on the reasons why the individual ingests faeces.

One of the most focused and effective ways of identifying when, what and how a behaviour happens is by using FBA. This approach can be used by parents as well as caregivers and professionals to assess and modify or change unwanted behaviours. For parents and caregivers, applying this 'theory' to dealing with eating faeces can enable them to desensitize themselves to the behaviour and be more positive about tackling the issue.

FBA involves parents and caregivers keeping careful diaries of three aspects of the behaviour:

- A: antecedent – what happens directly before the eating of faeces takes place? This should include where the behaviour happens.

- B: behaviour – what actually happened? Is it in the context of faecal smearing or some other pica behaviour? How long does the behaviour last, does the person ingest (actually eat) the faeces, just hold them up towards the mouth for the parent or caregiver to see, or rub faeces into the teeth, mouth or face without eating them?

- C: consequence – What happens after the behaviour? How do parents and caregivers respond?

Diaries are important for parents and caregivers as well as any professionals who may be involved in assessing and supporting behaviour change in an individual. Keeping diaries may seem onerous to parents and caregivers, especially if they are managing other difficult behaviours or other family commitments, but this form of documentation is critical in trying to reduce or eliminate ingestion of faeces.

In some cases, if this behaviour is one among several unwanted behaviours, it may be necessary to prioritize which behaviour to address first and deal with them one at a time. FBA can be used for a range of behaviours, so documenting the 'ABC' of each behaviour is the basis of changing them.

Causes of eating faeces

FBA may show one or more of the following to be causes of ingesting faeces:

- sensory issues
- social responses (how others react)
- inadvertent (unintended) rewards
- access to a desired object or activity
- avoidance of a situation or activity
- emotional issues.

SENSORY ISSUES

Sensory perceptual and sensory processing issues affect many people across the autism spectrum as well as others with intellectual and developmental conditions (Kern *et al.* 2006). This means that messages sent to the brain relating to the following senses are not functioning correctly:

- hearing (auditory)
- sight (visual)
- touch (tactile)
- taste (gustatory)
- smell (olfactory).

These five senses enable humans to make sense of the world by processing all the sensory stimulants in the environment. If sensory perception and processing is compromised, some individuals find sensory input, such as lighting, noises and colours, overwhelming. For example, they may struggle to manage in supermarkets where an array of sensations challenge their senses. Such individuals need reduced sensory input, gradually increased over time, to manage. Other individuals may be sensory deprived, so they attempt to increase sensory input by, for example, rocking, jumping or hitting themselves. Similarly to smearing, individuals who ingest faeces may do so to gain sensory input.

The feel of faeces to the touch and the intense odour and taste of faeces may fulfil their need for sensory input. Squeezing, rolling, licking and chewing faeces can prove enormously satisfying to the individual who is sensory deprived. Some individuals gravitate towards foods with particular textures or colours and they may refuse to eat anything that has a different colour and texture to their own faeces.

In order to tackle the sensory aspects of eating faeces it may be necessary to find an alternative to faeces for the individual. This may seem a backwards step to some parents and caregivers.

> When he was about five or six we had some support from the learning disability service but they're useless... They were talking about things like trying to give him...play dough which didn't make the slightest bit of difference. Various 'try this sensory stuff'...none of it made a difference. Because none of it could replicate... What they produced didn't mimic, it didn't have the smell, it didn't have the right feel... Unless you produce fake poo, but then what's the point of that because it is poo without the germs in it. Replace it with [fake] poo, it's like where do we go from here?
>
> Mother of 18-year-old young man with autism, cerebral palsy, intellectual and developmental disabilities

This mother expressed her feeling that fake faeces had no function, but it does eliminate the health risk of infection in the individual and others. The individual may start to feel better when, perhaps, she has been unable to express feeling unwell due to ingesting faeces. The stress on parents and caregivers will be reduced because of the lessened risk to health and they can then start to address eating faeces with less emotion. In addition, fake faeces have been shown to reduce ingestion of real faeces (Ing et al. 2011).

One study used artificial faeces as a safe alternative to real faeces in an intractable case when an individual continually ate faeces (Ing et al. 2011). This is the recipe for imitation faeces from Dr H. Roane on the research team:

You mix a little bit of flour and water together so the water is fairly opaque, but still liquid. Then add food coloring to the mix until it's the color you want (I think it's a lot of red, green and yellow to make brown). After that, just add flour until it makes a dough that you can knead and shape. (Personal communication 2016)

The resulting dough is moulded into stool-shaped pieces of 2.5 to 8 cm in length. However, these researchers didn't try to imitate the smell or taste of faeces, which might further improve the ability to distract the individual from real faeces. Creating a similar sensory stimulus to faeces might require strong flavours such as:

- yeast extract
- vinegar
- horseradish
- highly spiced foods
- mustard.

This will entail a time of trial and error as alternatives are tested out. Many of the suggested foods are 'hot' so parents and caregivers need to observe for heartburn as a possible side-effect of regularly consuming spicy foods. Once located, the alternative could be timetabled into the individual's day when eating faeces usually happens, such as when the individual is alone, according to diaries kept as part of the FBA. If ingesting faeces takes place when the individual is in the toilet room, the alternative may have to be available near the toilet or given to the individual as she sits there.

SOCIAL RESPONSES
As with smearing, the reaction of parents and caregivers to the behaviour can induce repeat episodes if the individual gets a strong response. Although it may make parents and caregivers temporarily feel better by demonstrating their emotions, such as by shouting or yanking the individual's hands away from her mouth, these responses, although negative, can reinforce the ingestion of faeces: the opposite of what parents and caregivers want.

Eating faeces is one form of pica in which ignoring the behaviour is not a viable option to reduce its incidence, because of the risks of infection and illness to the individual. However, a low-key response to each episode is still possible, so parents and caregivers should try to:

- avoid direct eye contact

- keep a 'flat' unemotional voice

- keep a neutral facial expression

- limit talking to giving instructions

- remove others from the situation, such as siblings, or other residents in supported living communities

- avoid body language that gives away emotion, such as aggressive posturing.

Low-key responses attempt to prevent the individual from gaining a reward, even inadvertently, from unwanted behaviours. In between any episodes of ingesting faeces, parents and caregivers should give as much positive feedback to the individual as possible. Even if the individual cannot speak, positive commentary on whatever the individual does is vital, such as commenting on 'good trying' to do a desired behaviour, such as sitting upright to eat a meal or holding a spoon, which may be combined with a smiley face card, a thumbs-up or a hug.

INADVERTENT (UNINTENDED) REWARDS

Sometimes it may be difficult not to reinforce ingesting faeces with what the individual perceives as 'rewards'. For example, if eating faeces is combined with ingesting other objects, this may cause intestinal obstruction or some other injury that warrants urgent medical treatment, and the individual may feel rewarded because of the appearance of medical staff or an ambulance. The way around this is not to refuse medical treatment but to reinforce with praise, positive feedback and attention when the individual is doing desired behaviours, and adopt low-key responses when they're engaging in pica. It's important that parents and caregivers do not expect instant results; resolving this behaviour may takes months or years depending partly on how entrenched the behaviour has become.

ACCESSING A DESIRED OBJECT OR ACTIVITY

The FBA may show that the individual is ingesting faeces because it results in her reliably being given a desired object or activity, which can be anything from a drink to a handheld electronic device such as an iPad (CBF 2013). The individual has learned that eating faeces, or even attempting to, gives her something she wants. It may not be possible for the child to have continuous access to the desired object and, indeed, it may not be healthy for the individual. For example, the individual may solely want a computer game to the negation of all other activities. Schedules can help individuals to do several activities and to work towards a desired activity.

Working on communication skills will teach the individual to ask for what she wants, even if the request consists of holding up a picture card, pointing at an image, signing or pressing a button.

AVOIDING AN UNWANTED SITUATION OR ACTIVITY

Again the FBA might identify that the individual is removed from particular situations if she ingests faeces (CBF 2013). For example, if the individual digs in a nappy/diaper and licks the faeces off the fingers, this may lead immediately to the person being moved away from other pupils in school and getting individual attention while she is cleaned.

The FBA itself should outline what happens directly before the ingestion of faeces, affording parents and caregivers information about what to look for as warning signs that the behaviour is going to occur and the opportunity to communicate with the individual about what she wants. This may be as simple as the individual holding up a card with the word 'stop' on it to show that she wants to finish an activity. Keeping diary sheets about which activities or situations she does not like will enable parents and caregivers to work out if there is an issue with a particular activity or situation for her, meaning it can be modified.

EMOTIONAL REASONS FOR EATING FAECES

The FBA may flag up emotional reasons for eating faeces, such as boredom or anxiety, which should be addressed individually.

- Boredom can be addressed by scheduling activities into the individual's day.

- Anxiety can be reduced by scheduling, limiting change and allowing notice of changes to schedules or what the individual is expecting to happen.

- Some case studies have shown that ingestion of faeces and other forms of pica may be used by the individual to gain attention, in the absence of any other means of requesting this (Addison 2013). Eating faeces causes parents and caregivers to try to ensure the safety of individuals, for example, to prevent choking or to remove the faeces from the mouth to reduce the likelihood of infections. This form of stressed, protective behaviour can be positive for the individual who may want interaction with others. Loneliness can be tackled by increasing activities and involvement with other people and having as low key a response as possible when pica does happen.

- Eating faeces may be an expression of frustration, which can be addressed through focusing on communication skills.

- Wanting to be alone. Some studies have highlighted cases where an individual develops ingestion of faeces or putting faeces into the mouth as a means of deterring caregivers from interrupting the individual's time alone. Doubtless these behaviours tend to reduce the willingness of others to interact with individuals, thereby giving them their own space. By developing better forms of communication with which individuals can indicate when they want to be alone (Addison 2013), giving them a sense of control and a voice, faeces-related behaviours may be reduced or eliminated.

Positive reinforcement

This part of the strategy enables an individual to learn about consequences in a positive way. So the individual gains a sensory 'high' by, for example, being given a favoured snuggle toy, alternative favourite food, time on the computer or time with a lava lamp, if she does not ingest faeces (or other examples of pica). The notion of consequence can be underpinned by narrative pictures, a picture board or using a computer, according to what the individual is used to when communicating, so the individual makes the connection between her behaviour and an object or activity she likes.

Over time the individual should slowly be weaned off or have fewer 'rewards'. This may be particularly important when individuals occupy most of their time with pica, and ingesting faeces when available. Again this is trial and error and may need the rewards to be reintroduced then slowly withdrawn again.

Discrimination training

This is an important aspect of reducing or eliminating eating faeces or other pica. Sometimes an individual may not be aware that some things are not to be eaten, that they are inedible (Haoui et al. 2003). This may be the case when individuals have sensory perception and processing issues. They may have heightened awareness of the sense of touch and taste and may perceive their world through the use of these senses, which may be distorted; thus they may touch and taste everything they meet in life, much as a very young child does. Discrimination training helps the individual to understand that some objects are not edible.

Depending on the cognitive skills of the individual, work could be done to distinguish between objects that can be eaten and those that cannot. This might entail using picture cards of, say, a tree, a hammer and an apple and working with the individual to post the cards into one of two boxes, one marked with a red circle and 'do not eat' and the other marked with a green circle and 'eat' on it. It is critical to include objects that the individual favours, for instance cigarette butts and faeces, to show that these are not for consumption.

Sensory activity

Additionally, sensory equipment should be made available to replace the need for ingestion of faeces and pica. Long term, the goal is to wean the individual off non-nutritive objects, so sensory toys or equipment could be made freely available in a box or in a sensory room with free access. The objects in the box or room should have similar characteristics to those the individual likes but which don't present the danger to health in terms of possible poisoning, introducing infections, choking and intestinal blockages.

It is possible to create play dough 'poop' which has the texture, size and smell of the faeces the individual usually consumes (see above). This may sound as if it is defeating the object of reducing or stopping the behaviour but it is a step towards improving the health of the individual. Additionally, research has shown positive results using imitation faeces as a means of ameliorating ingestion of faeces (Hagopian and Adelinis 2001; Ing et al. 2011).

Over time, access to the box or room of sensory items can be slowly limited. At the same time, other activities should be increased to create alternatives for the individual.

Distracting from eating faeces

The FBA will inform this strategy by telling parents and caregivers under what circumstances an individual ingests faeces. This may seem obvious, such as when they are alone on the toilet, but as with smearing, it may occur when the individual is alone in bed. In this case, placing easily accessible alternative activities by the bed, keeping music on, leaving a box of foods, low lighting, removing curtains/drapes, and so on may all distract the individual from ingesting faeces.

Alternative oral stimulation

Individuals who eat faeces gain oral stimulation and satisfaction from the process of chewing and moving objects around their mouths (Haoui et al. 2003). Some commentators suggest chewing gum may act as an alternative to faeces, which may be tempting, but it is

likely to be swallowed – and quickly – so may not reduce
or temporarily eliminate the pica behaviour. There are
therapeutic chewing devices, for example theratubing,
which are made of rubber of varying thicknesses. These
may need to be dipped in pungent and strongly flavoured
food substances to satisfy the individual's sensation
of taste.

Other interventions and future research

Some researchers have attempted to use a method
called 'response blocking' to alter pica behaviour. In
experimental conditions and with observers watching
the process, therapists consistently blocked all attempts
by individuals to pick up non-nutritive objects and insert
them into their mouths. This may seem a logical way
to try to stop pica. However, results have shown that
response blocking:

- may induce aggression in the individual
  (Hagopian and Adelinis 2001) and can cause
  the parent/caregiver relationship with the
  individual to become confrontational

- is even more person-intensive than monitoring
  pica behaviour to prevent injury or choking

- is not particularly effective (McCord et al. 2005)
  without other supportive interventions such
  as redirecting the individual to an alternative
  favoured food item (Hagopian and Adelinis 2001)

- has to be initiated at a very early point in the
  pica episode and must be absolutely consistent
  in each blocking response (McCord et al. 2005).

Reward systems may be useful if the individual
can understand and engage in the concept of reward
charts, or understand that there are instant rewards

for particular behaviours. When reward systems are combined with picture narratives, research cases have shown success in significantly reducing smearing and ingestion of faeces. In one study, smearing/eating behaviours were reduced to nil when the behaviours were purposefully ignored within safe levels (Kern *et al.* 2006).

It also has been suggested that, for individuals with the cognitive abilities to respond, cognitive behavioural therapy with a specialist behaviourist or psychological counsellor may have positive results (Haoui *et al.* 2003).

School plays a major role in a child's life and liaison with school over difficult behaviours is imperative for consistent support for the individual. Pica and eating faeces should be documented on the child's record (the education, health and care (EHC) plan in the UK), noting that 1:1 supervision is essential to prevent injury such as choking, and potential infection and illness from ingesting faeces, or from contaminating surfaces which others might touch. Parents and caregivers can document emergency hospital visits or incidents of ingestion of faeces which might evidence the need for 1:1 support. The same is true for adults with intellectual and developmental disabilities who engage in pica and should have this information documented in the individual's care plan and person-centred plan.

There are also the following sources of support:

- family doctor for referral

- autism consultant

- sensory processing occupational therapist

- speech therapist

- dentist for treatment of damage to teeth from chewing on inedible objects, for cleaning teeth and checking the mouth for oral infections

- social worker for community programmes
- dietitian.

For a list of agencies in the UK, the US and Australia see Appendix 1.

Insurance

For countries that do not have a socialized system of health care such as the UK's National Health Service (NHS), health insurance may cover ingestion of faeces and possibly dental treatment related to pica.

Medical insurance may cover coprophagia so long as it is diagnosed as pica, which itself is a form of eating disorder. Pica, described as eating non-nutritive objects, usually must have been present for at least one month and the individual must be older than two years of age, before which pica may be developmentally 'normal'.

Additionally, episodes of infection caused by ingesting faeces lead to the possibility of pica being categorized as 'failure to thrive' for the purposes of insurance.

Finally, some research has categorized all pica as 'self-injurious behaviour' (McCord *et al.* 2005) which may be covered by mental health insurance.

EASY-READ SUMMARY

Some people eat or taste faeces, sometimes with smearing. They may enjoy the strong smell and taste of faeces, so parents and caregivers can try giving them other strongly flavoured foods. Other people may like the reactions they get from eating faeces, so parents and caregivers should try not to show how they feel about the behaviour. Some mental health problems, such as OCD, make people want to eat faeces and keep them eating it.

For other people, eating faeces may get them out of things they don't want to do or a situation they don't want to be in. This can be worked out by keeping diaries of what happens at the time of the eating, then trying to change things to help the person get what they want without having to eat faeces.

Eating faeces is a bit like other eating of things that aren't food (pica). Parents and caregivers can help the person to work out the difference between foods to eat and things that are not foods. If this doesn't work, the person may eat fake or pretend faeces which is mainly made from flour and water so won't make the person ill.

5

Recurrence of Smearing and/or Ingesting Faeces

Locating the reasons

Medical

If recurrence happens, the first thing to exclude is a medical or physical cause of the behaviour. From adolescence onwards, individuals may develop chronic bowel conditions, such as Crohn's disease or ulcerative colitis, or genitourinary conditions, such as urinary infections, which can cause inflammation or other symptoms which may provoke scratching or rubbing the anal opening and lead to smearing and/or ingesting faeces (Kastner, Walsh and Fraser 2001). These conditions warrant medical investigation and treatment which might reduce or remove faecal-related behaviours. Even if an individual already has one diagnosis related to his smearing, he may develop other conditions or a worsening of the initial condition, both of which can be helped by medical assessment and treatment.

Constipation may recur, leading to a recurrence of smearing and possibly ingestion of faeces. Bowel activity will need monitoring to assess how effective medical treatment has been and to ensure constipation does not happen repeatedly. It is a myth that prescribed drugs for constipation cause the bowel to become 'lazy', leading to further constipation, so parents and caregivers should continue with medication as prescribed once a reassessment has been made by a medical practitioner.

Smearing and ingestion of faeces may recur because initial episodes have not been successfully addressed. For example, medical conditions may not have been assessed by a doctor, or treatment may not have been effective, or the condition may have worsened or be cyclical in nature.

Psychiatric

If previous episodes of smearing or eating faeces were thought to be due to psychiatric causes, these conditions may have worsened or the treatment may need to be increased for an effective dose for the individual. Additionally, new psychiatric conditions may have developed, one of the most common being anxiety-based conditions which are frequent in people with autism and ADHD, or the individual may have developed OCD of which smearing is thought to be a part.

Individuals who have not previously been diagnosed with any psychiatric illness may develop such conditions, for instance when they reach puberty. In older women, the menopause may be closely linked with developing panic disorder or panic attacks (Pacchierotti *et al.* 2004).

If sexual exploitation or abuse occurs, the individual may have post-traumatic stress disorder which can manifest as smearing.

Psychiatric conditions are related to smearing and eating faeces for the following reasons:

- They may cause psychosomatic itching of the anus, leading to scratching and smearing/eating faeces.

- They may interfere with the process of teaching toilet skills, which may take years with some individuals; successful toilet training can reduce or stop smearing.

- Certain factors during the life cycle can cause clinical insomnia, allowing opportunistic smearing/eating faeces at night.

Emotional and other reasons

It can be distressing for parents and caregivers if smearing and/or ingesting recurs and it can induce many negative emotions. Once again, the behaviours must be seen as having meaning, as being a way of communicating something that the individual cannot express in other ways. In other words, the individuals, too, are distressed and smearing is an expression of that.

Sometimes the reasons for renewed smearing may be different to the causes of the initial episode(s) so may be less obvious to parents and caregivers. The most likely causes are as follows:

- Changes to the individual's routines, particularly if these have been unexpected, prolonged or simply not wanted.

- Sometimes smearing behaviours can lead to tasting and then ingesting faeces.

- Illness can precede a recurrence of smearing or ingesting, which may be comforting and familiar behaviours.

- Loss can precipitate seemingly challenging behaviours which bring comfort to individuals. Loss may be the death of a parent or pet, or leaving one trusted and familiar situation for another, such as moving schools and missing or 'losing' teachers and support staff.

- Moving home may also precede smearing because the home is a physical manifestation of predictability and routine in the individual's life. This experience can make the individual extremely anxious, even if parents and caregivers have given support in terms of visual aids to show a house move, photos of the new home and a long lead-in to the changes.

- Renewed smearing may be a sign of neglect, for example if the individual is not being enabled to wash or clean up promptly after soiling.

- Returning to smearing and/or ingesting faeces may indicate sexual, emotional or physical abuse.

- If renewed smearing occurs after puberty, the individual may be physically exploring, using faeces as a lubricant, or be sexually aroused by fingering the anus.

Returning to a familiar behaviour can be as comforting during distressing times for individuals with intellectual and developmental disabilities as it is for those without. A clear example of this is when typically developed people comfort eat for a period when life is complicated or difficult.

Reintroducing toilet training

I can almost hear the groan from parents and caregivers who feel they've tried everything, the smearing returns and they are told to go back to toilet training with the individual. This book should contain a few extra pieces of information about toilet training which you may not have tried before, and it is the case that toilet training skills are a main way of addressing faeces-related behaviours.

If there is recurrence, it is tempting to return to what may have felt like tried and tested ways of managing these behaviours, such as nappies/diapers and restrictive clothing. However, although these measures may help parents and caregivers feel in control of the situation, they are at best short-term stress relievers for parents and caregivers, not for the individual.

Well-being of parents and caregivers

Recurrence of smearing and ingestion of faeces can cause parents and caregivers to feel depressed, hopeless or even angry. Some parents may consider this behaviour as a 'final straw' and have the individual moved out of the family home and into care.

Parents and caregivers may not have had any support during the initial episodes of the behaviours so it's important that they get support and resources from the appropriate agencies (see Appendix 1).

EASY-READ SUMMARY

Some people start to smear or eat faeces again after not doing it for some time. There are many reasons for this, such as stress and worry: the person likes to smear or eat faeces because he enjoys it or gets comfort from it. The person may start smearing or eating again because of medical problems either starting or coming back, like Crohn's disease and constipation. The person may have a mental illness. It's important to try to help the person out of nappies/diapers so he learns to use the toilet, which can stop smearing.

Appendix 1

Agencies

United Kingdom

The National Autistic Society

This is a charity that supports people on the autism spectrum and their families, as well as professionals and support staff working in this field. They provide information, including a helpline, training and support services.

Telephone: 0808 800 4104
www.autism.org.uk

The British Institute of Learning Disabilities (BILD)

BILD is a charity that addresses issues for people with learning disabilities, with a stated aim of enabling them to engage in society fully and with equality. BILD provides support to people with learning disabilities and their families as well as training and support for professionals and other staff in the field.

Telephone: 0121 415 6960
www.bild.org.uk

The Challenging Behaviour Foundation (CBF)

The focus of this charity is people with complex and severe learning disabilities who engage in so-called challenging behaviours. The charity provides information for families as well as professionals and other staff through training and by facilitating peer support.

Telephone: 01634 838739
www.challengingbehaviour.org.uk

MIND

This is a charity for those with mental health issues, providing information and support to individuals, families and professionals.

Telephone: 0300 123 3393
www.mind.org.uk

NHS Choices

How to get help for incontinence issues.

www.nhs.uk/Livewell/incontinence/Pages/Gettinghelp. aspx

US

The American Association on Intellectual and Developmental Disabilities (AAIDD)

This organization addresses issues for those with intellectual and developmental disabilities, giving national support and global leadership.

http://aaidd.org

The Arc

This organization has chapters throughout the US and supports people with intellectual and developmental disabilities.

www.thearc.org/learn-about/intellectual-disability

The Autism Society

With over 100 groups across the US, this charity promotes the welfare of those with autism and supports individuals and families.

www.autism-society.org

National Association for Continence
This charity provides education and support to those involved in any aspect of incontinence, either as an individual affected, families or professionals.

www.nafc.org/diaries

Australia
The Australasia Society for Intellectual Disability (ASID)
This charity seeks to improve the quality of life for those with intellectual disabilities through providing information.

www.asid.asn.au

Autism Spectrum Australia (Aspect)
This charity provides services for people with autism and their families.

www.autismspectrum.org.au

Continence Foundation of Australia
This charity provides resources to individuals, their families and professionals to manage bladder and bowel issues.

www.continence.org.au

Appendix 2

Diagnostic Criteria

Oppositional defiant disorder

This is diagnosed when an individual displays four or more of the following behaviours for at least six months and directed towards individuals who are not a sibling:

- a predominantly angry mood, demonstrated by frequent bouts of temper about seemingly little

- behaviours which show defiance and argumentativeness to an extreme, often involving breaking the law or defying those in authority

- vindictive behaviours which do not abate or reduce in potency over time.

Some of these behaviours are apparent in us all but it is the intensity and frequency that earmark these as pathological and requiring psychiatric support. The behaviours happen in numerous settings, inflicting distress on family members and others in the individual's social circle. These behaviours may occur at home, in work or in recreational and social settings and may be associated with other psychiatric conditions, such as clinical depression, psychosis and bipolar disorder.

Conduct disorder

This is a pattern of behaviours which defy social rules and mores, are present for a minimum of 12 months and include at least one of the following in the previous six months:

- cruelty and physical/emotional aggression to other people and animals
- damaging property
- stealing and deceit
- breaking rules.

These behaviours are persistent and extreme. They violate the rights of others in numerous settings in the individual's life and impact significantly on that person's abilities to function socially, to be employed and to study.

References

Addison, M. (2013) *Information Sheet: Finding the Cause of Challenging Behaviour: Part 2.* Chatham: The Challenging Behaviour Foundation.

Ali, Z. (2001) Pica in people with intellectual disability: A literature review of aetiology, epidemiology and complications. *Journal of Intellectual and Developmental Disability 26:* 205–215.

American Psychiatric Association (APA) (2014) *Diagnostic and Statistical Manual of Mental Disorders, Fifth Edition (DSM-5).* Washington, DC: APA.

Azrin, N.H. and Foxx, R.M. (1971) A rapid method of toilet training the institutionalized retarded. *Journal of Applied Behavior Analysis 2*(4): 89–99.

Bainbridge, N. and Smith Myles, B. (1999) The use of priming to introduce toilet training to a child with autism. *Focus on Autism and Other Developmental Disabilities 14*(2): 106–109. Cited in Hayward, B. (2010) *Practice Guide: Reducing the Use of Restrictive Clothing as Mechanical Restraint: Supporting People to Achieve Dignity Without Restraints.* Office of the Senior Practitioner, State Government Victoria, Australia.

Barltrop, D. (1966) The prevalence of pica. *American Journal of Diseases of Children 112:* 116–123.

Beare, P.L., Severson, S. and Brandt, P. (2004) The use of a positive approach to increase engagement on-task activities and decrease challenging behaviour. *Behaviour Modification 28*(1): 28–44.

Beck, D.A. and Frohberg, N.R. (2005) Coprophagia in an elderly man: A case report and review of the literature. *International Journal of Psychiatry Medicine 35:* 417–427.

Benninga, M.A. (2004) Children with constipation: What happens to them when they grow up? *Scandinavian Journal of Gastroenterology 241:* 23–26.

Bernard, C. (1999) Child sexual abuse and the black disabled child. *Disability and Society 14:* 325–339.

Bohmer, C.J., Taminiau, J.A., Klinkenberg-Knol, E.C. and Meuwissen, S.G. (2001) The prevalence of constipation in institutionalized people with intellectual disability. *Journal of Intellectual Disability Research 45:* 212–218.

Bouras, N. and Drummond, C. (1992) Behavior and psychiatric disorders of people with mental handicaps living in the community. *Journal of Intellectual Disability Research 36:* 349–357.

Brahm, N.C., Buswell, A.L., Brahm, R.E. and Brown, R.C. (2004) Protozoal infections in the developmentally disabled: often overlooked cause of rectal digging and faecal smearing. *Annals of Pharmacotherapy 38(9)*: 1542.

Brahm, N.C., Farmer, K.C. and Brown, R.C. (2007) Risperidone for the treatment of fecal smearing in a developmentally disabled adult. *American Journal of Health Systems Pharmacy 64*: 382–384.

Carlson, J.I., Luiselli, J.K., Slyman, A. and Markowski, A. (2008) Choice-making as intervention for public disrobing in children with developmental disabilities. *Journal of Positive Behaviour Interventions 10(2)*: 86–90.

Carr, E. and Smith, C. (1995) Biological setting events for self-injury. *Mental Retardation and Developmental Disabilities Research Reviews 1*: 94–98.

Carr, E.G., Horner, R.H., Turnbull, A.P., Marquis, J.G. *et al.* (1999) *Positive Behavior Support for People with Developmental Disabilities: A Research Synthesis* (American Association on Mental Retardation Monograph Series). Washington, DC: American Association on Mental Retardation.

Carroll, K.E. and Kincade, D.H. (2007) Inclusive design in apparel product development for working women with physical disabilities. *Family and Consumer Sciences Research Journal 35(4)*: 289–315.

Cascio, C., McGlone, F., Folger, S., Tannan, V. *et al.* (2008) Tactile perception in adults with autism: A multidimensional psychophysical study. *Journal of Autism and Developmental Disorders 38*: 127–137.

Case, J. and Konstantareas, M.M. (2011) Interventions for inappropriate handling of feces in adults with autism spectrum disorders abstract. *Journal of Developmental Disabilities 17(2): 73–79.*

Challenging Behaviour Foundation (CBF) (2013) *Information Sheet: Pica (Eating Inedible Objects).* The Challenging Behaviour Foundation. Available at   www.challengingbehaviour.org.uk/understanding-behaviour/pica-polydipsia-sheet.html, accessed on 16 August 2016.

Coleman, J. and Spurling, G. (2010) Constipation in people with learning disability. *British Medical Journal 340*: c222.

Cooke, P. and Standen, P.J. (2002) Abuse and disabled children: Hidden needs...? *Child Abuse Review 11*: 1–18.

Cusack, J., Shaw, S., Spiers, J. and Sterry, R. (2016) *Personal tragedies, public crisis: the urgent need for a national response to early death in autism.* Autistica. Available   at   www.autistica.org.uk/wp-content/uploads/2016/03/ Personal-tragedies-public-crisis.pdf, accessed on 21 September 2016.

Dalrymple, N.J. and Ruble, L.A. (1992) Toilet training and behaviours of people with autism: Parent views. *Journal of Autism and Developmental Disorders 22(2)*: 265–275.

Decker, C.J. (1993) Pica in the mentally handicapped: A 15-year surgical perspective. *Canadian Journal of Surgery 36*: 551–554.

Del Giudice, E., Staiano, A., Capano, G., Romano, A. *et al.* (1999) Gastrointestinal manifestations in children with cerebral palsy. *Brain Development 21:* 307–311.

Dharmarajan, T.S., Gunturu, S.G. and Pitchumoni, C.S. (2012) *Geriatric Gastroenterology.* New York, NY: Springer Publishing.

Dickstein, D.P. (2010) Oppositional defiant disorder. *Journal of the American Academy Child and Adolescent Psychiatry 49(5):* 435–436.

Didden, R., Duker, P.C. and Korzilius, H. (1997) Meta-analytic study on treatment effectiveness for problem behaviors with individuals who have mental retardation. *American Journal on Mental Retardation 101:* 387–399.

Donnellan, C.A. and Playfer, J.R. (1999) A case of coprophagia presenting with sialadenitis. *Age Ageing 28(2):* 233–234.

Ducker, P.C. and Dekkers, M. (1992) Development of diurnal bladder control in severely and profoundly mentally handicapped residents. *Journal of Intellectual Disability Research 36:* 177–181.

Dudley, J.R., Ahlgrim-Delzell, L. and Calhoun, M.L. (1999) Diverse diagnostic and behavioural patterns amongst people with a dual diagnosis. *Journal of Intellectual Disability Research 43:* 70–79.

Eastland, R. (2001) *The role of zinc in Downs Syndrome.* Available at www.dsrf-uk.org/library/documents/The_Role_of_Zinc_in_Downs_Syndrome.pdf, accessed on 21 September 2016.

Edwards, C.H. (1959) Clay and cornstarch eating women. *Journal of American Dietetic Association 35:* 810–815.

Elawad, M.A. and Sullivan, P.B. (2001) Management of constipation in children with disabilities. *Developmental Medicine and Child Neurology 43:* 829–832.

Emerson, E. and Baines, S. (2010) *Health Inequalities and People with Learning Disabilities in the UK: 2010.* London: DOH.

Evans, P. and Brunsell, S. (2007) Uterine fibroid tumors: Diagnosis and treatment. *American Family Physician 75(10):* 1503–1508.

Fleming, E. and MacAlister, L. (2016) *Toilet Training and the Autism Spectrum (ASD): A Guide for Professionals.* London: Jessica Kingsley Publishers.

Foxx, R.M. and Martin, E.D. (1975) Treatment of scavenging behavior (coprophagy and pica) by overcorrection. *Behavior Research and Therapy 13:* 153–162.

Friedin, B.D. and Johnson, H.K. (1979) Treatment of a retarded child's faeces smearing and coprophagic behaviour. *Journal of Mental Deficiency Research 23(1):* 55–61.

Grandin, T. and Scariano, M.M. (1986) *Emergence: Labeled Autistic. A True Story.* New York: Grand Central Publishing.

Gray, C. (2010) *The New Social Story Book.* Arlington, TX: Future Horizons.

Hagopian, L.P. and Adelinis, J.D. (2001) Response blocking with and without redirection for the treatment of pica. *Journal of Applied Behavior Analysis 34*: 527–530.

Haoui, R., Gautie, L. and Puisset, F. (2003) Pica: a descriptive study of patients in a speciality medical center. *Encephale 29*(5): 415–424.

Hartman, D. (2013) *Sexuality and Relationship Education for Children and Adolescents with Autism Spectrum Disorders: A Professional's Guide to Understanding, Preventing Issues, Supporting Sexuality and Responding to Inappropriate Behaviours.* London: Jessica Kingsley Publishers.

Hartman, D. (2015a) *The Growing Up Book for Boys: What Boys on the Autism Spectrum Need to Know!* London: Jessica Kingsley Publishers.

Hartman, D. (2015b) *The Growing Up Guide for Girls: What Girls on the Autism Spectrum Need to Know!* London: Jessica Kingsley Publishers.

Hayward, B. (2010) *Reducing the Use of Restrictive Clothing as Mechanical Restraint: Supporting People to Achieve Dignity without Restraints.* Office of the Senior Practitioner, State Government Victoria, Australia.

Heslop, P., Fleming, P., Hoghton, M., Russ, L., Blair, P. and Marriott, A. (2013) *Confidential Inquiry into Premature Deaths of People with Learning Disabilities (CIPOLD): Final Report.* Norah Fry Centre for Disability Studies, University of Bristol.

Huntley, E. and Smith, L. (1999) Long-term follow-up of behavioural treatment for primary encopresis in people with intellectual disability in the community. *Journal of Intellectual Disability Research 43*(6): 484–488.

Ing, A.D., Roane, H.S. and Veenstra, R.A. (2011) Functional analysis and treatment of coprophagia. *Journal of Applied Behavioral Analysis 44*(1): 151–155.

Jancar, J. and Speller, C.J. (1994) Fatal intestinal obstruction in the mentally handicapped. *Journal of Intellect Disability Research 38*: 413–422.

Jawed, S.H., Krishnan, V.H., Prasher, V.P. and Corbett, J.A. (1993) Worsening of pica as a symptom of depressive illness in a person with severe mental handicap. *British Journal of Psychiatry 162*: 835–837.

Jones, D.J. (1992) ABC of colorectal diseases: Pruritus ani. *British Medical Journal 305*: 575–577.

Josephs, K.A., Whitwell, J.L., Parisi, J.E. and Lapid, M.I. (2016) Coprophagia in neurologic disorders. *Journal of Neurology 263*(5):1008–1014.

Kastner, T., Walsh, K.K. and Fraser, M. (2001) Undiagnosed medical conditions and medication side effects presenting as behavioral/psychiatric problems in people with mental retardation. *Mental Health Aspects of Developmental Disabilities 4*(3): 101–107.

Kern, J.K., Trivedi, M.H., Garver, C.R., Grannemann, B.D. *et al.* (2006) The pattern of sensory processing abnormalities in autism. *Autism 10*: 480–494.

Kinnell, H.G. (1985) Pica as a feature of autism. *British Journal of Psychiatry* 147: 80–82.

Knell, S.M. and Moore, D.J. (1990) Cognitive-behavioral play therapy in the treatment of encopresis. *Journal of Clinical Child Psychology* 19: 55–60.

Kral, T.V.E., Eriksen, W.T., Souders, M.C. & Pinto-Martin, J.A. (2013) Eating Behaviors, Diet Quality, and Gastrointestinal Symptoms in Children with Autism Spectrum Disorders: A brief review. *Journal of Pediatric Nursing* 28: 548–556.

Lancioni, G.E., O'Reilly, M.F., Serenelli, S. and Campodonico, F. (2000) Alarm signals and prompts to eliminate large urinary accidents in a woman with multiple disabilities. *Scandinavian Journal of Behaviour Therapy* 29(3–4): 152–155.

Lightfoot, E.B. and LaLiberte, T.L. (2006) Approaches to child protection case management for cases involving people with disabilities. *Child Abuse and Neglect* 30: 381–391.

Luiselli, J.K. (1997) Teaching toilet skills in a public school setting to a child with pervasive developmental disorder. *Journal of Behavior Therapy and Experimental Psychiatry* 28(2): 163–168.

Mackenzie-Keating, S.E. and McDonald, L. (1990) Overcorrection: reviewed, revisited and revised. *Journal of Behavioural Analysis* 13(1): 39–48.

Makaton Charity (2008) *Makaton Sex Education Book of Symbols*. The Makaton Charity Publications.

Matson, J.L., Belva, B., Hattier, M.A. and Matson, M.L. (2011) Pica in persons with developmental disabilities: Characteristics, diagnosis and assessment. *Research in Autism Spectrum Disorders* 5: 1459–1464.

Matson, J.L. and LoVulla, S.V. (2009) Encopresis, soiling and constipation in children and adults with developmental disability. *Research in Developmental Disabilities* 30: 799–807.

McCord, B.E., Grosser, J.W., Iwata, B.A. and Powers, L.A. (2005) An analysis of response-blocking parameters in the prevention of pica. *Journal of Applied Behavior Analysis* 38(3): 391–394.

McDonnell, A.A., Waters, T. and Jones, D. (2002) Low Arousal Approaches in the Management of Challenging Behaviours. In D. Allen (ed.) *Ethical Approaches to Physical Interventions: Responding to Challenging Behaviours in People with Intellectual Disabilities*. Plymouth: BILD.

McLoughlin, I.J. (1987) The picas. *British Journal of Hospital Medicine* 37: 286–290.

Mellon, M.W., Whiteside, S.P. and Freidrich, W.N. (1990) The relevance of fecal soiling as an indicator of child sexual abuse: a preliminary analysis. *Journal of Developmental and Behavioral Pediatrics* 27(1): 25–32.

Motta, R.W. and Basile, D.M. (1998) Pica. In L. Phelps (ed.) *Health-Related Disorders in Children: A Guidebook for Understanding and Educating*. Washington, DC: American Psychiatric Association.

Nagaratnam, N., Lim, W. and Hutyn, S. (2001) Some problematic behaviors in Alzheimer's dementia. *Archives of Gerontology and Geriatrics 32*(1): 57–65.

Nevala, N., Holopainen, J., Kinnunen, O. and Hanninen, O. (2003) Reducing the physical work load and strain of personnel helpers through clothing redesign. *Applied Ergonomics 34*: 557–563.

Neveus, T., Von Gontard, A., Hoebeke, P., Hjalmas, K. *et al.* (2006) The standardization of terminology of lower urinary tract function in children and adolescents: report from the Standardisation Committee of the International Children's Continence Society. *Journal of Urology 176*(1): 314–324.

NICE (2010) *Constipation in Children and Young People: Diagnosis and Management* (CG99). London: National Institute for Health and Care Excellence. Available at www.nice.org.uk/guidance/cg99/chapter/Key-priorities-for-implementation, accessed on 21 September 2016.

NICE (2014) *Pruritus Ani.* London: National Institute for Health and Care Excellence, Clinical Knowledge Summaries. Information published online, accessed 10 April 2014. Available at http://cks.nice.org.uk/pruritus-ani, accessed on 20 October 2016.

Nicholson, J.H., Morton, R.E., Attfield, S. and Rennie, D. (2001) Assessment of upper-limb function and movement in children with cerebral palsy wearing lycra garments. *Developmental Medicine and Child Neurology 43*(6): 384–391.

Nisbett, D.J. and Johnson, K.K.P. (1992) Clothing fashionability and students with a disability: Impression of social and mental competencies. *Clothing and Textiles Research Journal 11*(1): 39–44.

O'Brien, G. and Whitehouse, A. (1990) A psychiatric study of deviant eating behaviour among mentally handicapped adults. *British Journal of Psychiatry 157*: 281–284.

Pacchierotti, C., Castrogiovanni, A., Cavicchioli, C., Luisi, S. *et al.* (2004) Panic disorder in menopause: A case control study. *Maturitas 48*(2): 147–154.

Pardini, M. and Guida, S. (2010) Aripiprazole treatment for coprophagia in autistic disorder. *Journal of Neuropysychiatry and Clinical Neurosciences 22*(4): 451.

Parry-Jones, B. and Parry-Jones, W.L. (1992) Pica: symptom or eating disorder? A historical assessment. *British Journal of Psychiatry 160*: 341–354.

Piazza, C.C., Fisher, W.W., Hanley, G.P., LeBlanc, L.A. *et al.* (1998) Treatment of pica through multiple analyses of its reinforcing functions. *Journal of Applied Behavior Analysis 31*: 165–189.

Powers, R.E. (2005) *Medical and Psychiatric Management of Fecal Smearing in Persons with Mental Retardation and Developmental Disabilities (MR/DD)* (DDMED 26). Bureau of Geriatric Psychiatry. Available at www.ddmed.org/pdfs/26.pdf, accessed on 21 September 2016.

Prasher, V.P. and Clarke, D.J. (1996) Case report: Challenging behaviour in a young adult with Down's syndrome and autism. *British Journal of Learning Disabilities 24*: 167–169.

Radford, L., Corral, S., Bradley, C., Fisher, H. *et al.* (2011) *Child Abuse and Neglect in the UK Today.* NSPCC. Available at www.nspcc.org.uk/services-and-resources/research-and-resources/pre-2013/child-abuse-and-neglect-in-the-uk-today, accessed on 20 October 2016

Rennie, D.J., Attfield, S.F., Morton, R.E., Polak, F.J. and Nicholson, J. (2000) An evaluation of lycra garments in the lower limb using 3-D gait analysis and functional assessment (PEDI). *Gait and Posture 12*: 1–6.

Reynolds, K.E. (2013) *Sexuality and Severe Autism: A Practical Guide for Parents, Caregivers and Health Educators.* London: Jessica Kingsley Publishers.

Reynolds, K.E. (2014) *Tom Needs to Go: A Book About How to Use Public Toilets Safely for Boys and Young Men with Autism and Related Conditions.* London: Jessica Kingsley Publishers.

Reynolds, K.E. (2015) *Ellie Needs to Go: A Book About How to Use Public Toilets for Girls and Young Women with Autism and Related Conditions.* London: Jessica Kingsley Publishers.

Rinald, K. and Mirenda, P. (2012) Effectiveness of a modified rapid toilet training workshop for parents of children with developmental disabilities. *Research in Developmental Disabilities: A Multidisciplinary Journal 33*(3): 933–943.

Roane, H.S, Kelly, M.L and Fisher, W.W. (2003) The effects of noncontingent access to food on the rate of object mouthing across three settings. *Journal of Applied Behavior Analysis 36*: 579–582.

Rojahn, J., Schroeder, S.R. and Mulick, J.A. (1980) Ecological assessment of self-protective devices in three profoundly retarded adults. *Journal of Autism and Developmental Disorders 10*(1): 59–66.

Rolider, A., Williams, L., Cummings, A. and van Houten, R. (1991) The use of a brief movement restriction procedure to eliminate severe inappropriate behavior. *Journal of Behavior Therapy and Experimental Psychiatry 22*(1): 23–30.

Roohani, N., Hurrell, R., Kelishadi, R and Schulin, R. (2013) Zinc and its importance for human health: An integrative review. *Journal of Research in Medical Sciences 18*(2): 144–157.

Rose, F., Porcerelli, J.H. and Neale, A.V. (2000) Pica: Common but commonly missed. *Journal of American Board of Family Practice 13*: 353–358.

Rubin, G. and Dale, A. (2006) Chronic constipation in children. *British Medical Journal 333*: 1051–1055.

Russell, A.J., Mataix-Cols, D., Anson, M. and Murphy, D.G.M. (2005) Obsessions and compulsions in Asperger syndrome and high-functioning autism. *British Journal of Psychiatry 186*(6): 525–528.

Schupf, N., Zigman, W., Lee, J.H., Kline, J. and Levin, B. (1997) Early menopause in women with Down's Syndrome. *Journal of Intellectual Disability Research 41*(3):264–267.

Scotti, J.R., Evans, I.M., Meyer, L.H. and Walker, P. (1991) A meta-analysis of intervention research with problem behaviour: Treatment validity and standards of practice. *American Journal on Mental Retardation 96*: 233–256.

Sequeira, H. and Hollins, S. (2003) Clinical effects of sexual abuse on people with learning disability: Critical literature review. *British Journal of Psychiatry 182*(1): 13–19.

Shakespeare, T. (2013) *Disability Rights and Wrongs Revisited*. Abingdon: Routledge.

Sinason, V. (2002) Treating people with learning disabilities after physical or sexual abuse. *Advances in Psychiatric Treatment 8*: 424–432.

Smith, L.J. (1996) A behavioural approach to the treatment of non-retentive encopresis in adults with learning disabilities. *Journal of Intellectual Disability Research 40*(2): 130–139.

Stancliff, B.L. (1999) A better fit. Apparel for persons with disabilities. *OT Practice 4*(2): 17–20.

Sullivan, P.B. (2008) Gastrointestinal disorders in children with neurodevelopmental disabilities. *Developmental Disabilities Research Reviews 14*: 128–136.

Tarbox, R.S.F., Williams, W.L. and Friman, P.C. (2004) Extended diaper wearing: Effects on continence in and out of the diaper. *Journal of Applied Behaviour Analysis 37*: 97–100.

Turgay, A. (2005) Treatment of comorbidity in conduct disorder with attention-deficit hyperactivity disorder (ADHD). *Essential Psychopharmacology 6*(5): 277–290.

Van Laecke, E. (2008) Elimination disorders in people with intellectual disability. *Journal of Intellectual Disability Research 52*(10): 810.

Von Gontard, A. (2013) Urinary incontinence in children with special needs. *Nature Reviews Urology 10*(11): 667–674.

Von Wendt, L., Similia, S., Niskanen, P. and Jarvelin, M.R. (1990) Development of bowel and bladder control in the mentally retarded. *Developmental Medicine and Child Neurology 32*: 515–518.

Warnke, M. (1991) *Schemes of Satan*. Tulsa, OK: Victory House, Inc.

Whelan Banks, J. (2008) *Liam Goes Poo in the Toilet: A Story about Trouble with Toilet Training*. London: Jessica Kingsley Publishers.

Williams, D. (2002) *Exposure Anxiety: The Invisible Cage*. London: Jessica Kingsley Publishers.

Index